SAINT JOHN CHRYSOSTOM

Letters to Saint Olympia

ST VLADIMIR'S SEMINARY PRESS
Popular Patristics Series
Number 56

The Popular Patristics Series published by St Vladimir's Seminary Press provides readable and accurate translations of a wide range of early Christian literature to a wide audience—students of Christian history to lay Christians reading for spiritual benefit. Recognized scholars in their fields provide short but comprehensive and clear introductions to the material. The texts include classics of Christian literature, thematic volumes, collections of homilies, letters on spiritual counsel, and poetical works from a variety of geographical contexts and historical backgrounds. The mission of the series is to mine the riches of the early Church and to make these treasures available to all.

Series Editor
BOGDAN BUCUR

Associate Editor
IGNATIUS GREEN

* * *

Series Editor
1999–2020
JOHN BEHR

SAINT JOHN CHRYSOSTOM

Letters to Saint Olympia

Translated, with an Introduction, by

DAVID C. FORD

ST VLADIMIR'S SEMINARY PRESS
YONKERS, NEW YORK
2016

Library of Congress Cataloging-in-Publication Data

Names: John Chrysostom, Saint, –407, author. | Ford, David, 1949– translator.
Title: Letters to Saint Olympia / Saint John Chrysostom ; translated, with an introduction, by David C. Ford.
Description: Yonkers, New York : St. Vladimir's Seminary Press, 2017. | Series: Popular Patristics series, ISSN 1555–5755 ; Number 56 | Includes bibliographical references and index.
Identifiers: LCCN 2016052539 (print) | LCCN 2016055662 (ebook) | ISBN 9780881415582 (paper) | ISBN 9780881415599 (e-book) | ISBN 9780881415599
Subjects: LCSH: John Chrysostom, Saint, –407—Correspondence. | Olympias, Saint, approximately 368–408—Correspondence. | Christian women—Religious life.
Classification: LCC BR65.C43 E5 2017 (print) | LCC BR65.C43 (ebook) | DDC 270.2092—dc23
LC record available at https://lccn.loc.gov/2016052539

ISBN 978-0-88141-558-2 (paper)
ISBN 978-0-88141-559-9 (electronic)
ISSN 1555-5755

PRINTED IN THE UNITED STATES OF AMERICA

*This book is dedicated to the parishioners of
St Olympia Orthodox Mission,
Potsdam, NY,
who started me on this wondrous project;*

*and to Gerondissa Olympiada,
Abbess of Holy Protection Orthodox Monastery,
White Haven, PA,
who is striving to guide her monastics
in the spirit of St Olympia.*

Table of Contents

Introduction

St John Chrysostom (*c.* 349–407), the author of these letters, is one of the greatest and most beloved of all the church fathers. Along with St Basil the Great and St Gregory the Theologian, he is venerated in the Orthodox Church as one of the Three Holy Hierarchs, whose joint feastday is January 30. His extensive, detailed exegetical preaching on many books of the Bible—especially the Gospels of Matthew and John, Acts, and the Pauline Epistles—makes him the greatest biblical commentator in the history of the Greek-speaking Church, and the spiritual depth and melodic eloquence of his sermons make him the greatest preacher in the history of Christianity, both in the East and in the West.

These remarkable letters were all written while Chrysostom was in exile—enduring the banishment that consumed the last three years of his life (404–407). He had been the archbishop of Constantinople, the capital city of the Roman Empire, from 398 to 404. Prior to that, as a priest, he was the main preacher for twelve years in the Great Church in Antioch, one of the greatest cities in the empire, where he was born and raised. It was the sheer beauty and spiritual power of his preaching in both of these cities that won him the epithet *Chrysostomos*, meaning "Golden Mouth."

It is unnecessary to rehearse Chrysostom's life in detail, as that has already been done elsewhere.[1] Much less is known about St

---

[1] The standard biography for many years was by Chrysostomus Baur, entitled *John Chrysostom and His Time* (Westminster, MD: The Newman Press, 1959). More recently, the noted scholar J. N. D. Kelly has written a full biography, entitled *Golden Mouth: The Story of John Chrysostom—Ascetic, Preacher, Bishop* (Grand Rapids, MI: Baker Books, 1995). Also, an eleven-page biographical introduction appears in my book entitled *Women and Men in the Early Church: The Full Views of St. John Chrysostom* (South Canaan, PA: St. Tikhon's Seminary Press, 1996), 1–11.

Olympia, the deaconess and abbess who played a major role in his life during his years as archbishop of Constantinople, and even—by long distance—during his three years of exile in the little town of Cucusus in eastern Asia Minor, located more than 400 miles overland from Constantinople. What follows is a brief summary of her life.

St Olympia's Life[2]

The little girl who would become the highly intelligent, devout, magnanimous, and rigorously ascetical St Olympia was born around the year 362 into a pagan family in the upper aristocracy of the imperial city of Constantinople. Her father, named Seleucus, was a count of the empire; her mother was named Alexandra.

Olympia's paternal grandfather was the Praetorian prefect and consul[3] Ablabius, who was a senator in the time of Emperor Constantine the Great (ruled 312–337). It was this Ablabius who amassed the stupendous fortune that would be passed down to Olympia.

Olympia's parents died when she was still young, so she was brought up under the guardianship of an uncle, named Procopius, who was a pious Christian, as was her governess, Theodosia. Together they raised her in the love and nurture of Christ, and through them she became closely connected with some major bishops and theologians in the Church. Theodosia was a sister of St Amphilochius, bishop of Iconium and a close friend of St Basil the Great, and

---

[2]The major source for her life is *The Life of Olympia*, an anonymous work which was written perhaps around the year 440 (given in French and Greek in SC 13 [2nd ed.], 406–49; and in English, in *Jerome, Chrysostom, and Friends,* Elizabeth Clark, ed. [New York: The Edwin Mellen Press, 1979], 127–44). There is also significant information about her in Bishop Palladius of Helenopolis, *Dialogue on the Life of St. John Chrysostom,* Robert T. Meyer, trans., ACW 45 (Westminster, MD: The Newman Press, 1985), 66–67, 104–16.

[3]These were high offices of authority in the administrative structure of the Roman Empire, although by the first half of the fourth century they had become mostly ceremonial positions of honor.

Procopius was a close friend of St Gregory the Theologian, who took a great interest in Olympia after he came to Constantinople in 379. At that time, even though she was only about seventeen years old, she became a benefactor of the Church of the Anastasia (the Resurrection) in the capital, where St Gregory preached his famous sermons against the Arians, which gained him the title "the Theologian."

At about the age of twenty-one, Olympia married a man of high rank named Nebridius. St Gregory could not attend the wedding due to ill health, so instead he wrote her a letter, along with a poem. In this poem (PG 37.1542–50), he refers to her as "a mirror of a Christian woman." Later, Olympia prompted St Gregory of Nyssa, St Basil the Great's younger brother and another of the great Cappadocian fathers, to write his *Commentary on the Song of Songs*, which he dedicated to her, as we can see from the opening words of this work:

> Greetings in the Lord, to the most worthy Olympia, from Gregory, Bishop of Nyssa. I have learned of your concern for the Song of Songs which you have expressed to me both in person and by your letters. . . . I have eagerly accepted your solicitude regarding this task. I do not offer you anything that would benefit your conduct, for I am persuaded that your soul's eye is pure from every passionate, unclean thought, and that it looks without hindrance at God's grace by means of these divine words of the Song.[4]

Thus, we see that Olympia was highly regarded by some of the great fathers of the Church before she became the closest friend and confidante of St John Chrysostom.

After a short period of married life lasting less than twenty months, Olympia's husband died, leaving her a young widow with an immense fortune, including estates in Thrace, Galatia, Cappadocia,

---

[4]St Gregory of Nyssa, *Commentary on the Song of Songs*, Casimir McCambley, trans. (Brookline, MA: Hellenic College Press, 1987), 35.

and Bithynia, as well as numerous properties in Constantinople itself. Since she was of the upper aristocracy, her situation came to the attention of Emperor Theodosius the Great (ruled 379–395), who naturally assumed that she should—and would want to—remarry. Indeed, he even selected a kinsman of his, named Elpidius, to be her new husband. However, she adamantly refused even to consider such a possibility. Instead, she dedicated the rest of her life to consecrated celibacy in service to the Church, thus becoming an even more generous supporter of the Church.

When Emperor Theodosius heard this, he ordered her vast properties to be held in trust for her until her thirtieth birthday, unless she agreed to the proposed marriage union. Still she refused, saying, as reported by Chrysostom's friend and biographer, Bishop Palladius of Helenopolis,

> You have demonstrated toward my lowly person a kindness most becoming an emperor and commendable in a bishop when you entrusted this great burden, which has been my worry, to proper administration. You will do much better should you order it to be distributed to the poor and the churches. I have been praying for quite a while that I be set free from the embarrassment of vainglory, which would be mine if I distributed it to charity. Let me not be so seduced by earthly things as to lose the soul's true riches.[5]

Perhaps appreciating the "spunkiness" of her reply, the emperor soon restored control of her inheritance to her, allowing her to dispose of her wealth as she saw fit.[6]

As W. R. W. Stephens writes,

---

[5] Palladius, *Dialogue on the Life of St. John Chrysostom*, 114.

[6] All of this, and what follows, shows that in the eastern Roman Empire (generally speaking, more so than in the West) it was considered appropriate for women to inherit property and administer it themselves, and to have significant influence in church affairs.

Henceforward her time and wealth were devoted to the service of the Christian religion. She ministered to the necessities of the sick and poor, and supported the work of the Church in Greece, Asia Minor, and Syria with such lavish donations, not only of her money but of her land, that even Chrysostom, who might be called the great preacher of almsgiving, warned her against indiscriminate liberality, reminding her that as her wealth was a trust committed to her by God, she ought to be discreet in the management of it.[7]

Some years before Chrysostom came from Antioch to Constantinople early in 398, Olympia established a monastery in a palace on one of her own properties, which directly adjoined the great cathedral in the city. She began to live a life of asceticism there, along with several relatives and about fifty of her former servants, to whom she had granted their freedom, and whom she directed and supervised as abbess of the monastery. In time, the monastery grew to house about 250 female ascetics.

Stephens describes her ascetic endeavors in these terms:

She practiced the most austere asceticism, renouncing the luxury of the bath [except for rare exceptions], wearing none but old, coarse clothing, and subjecting herself to severe restrictions in regard to food and sleep.[8]

Some time after turning thirty years old, Olympia was ordained as a deaconess by Archbishop Nectarius, Chrysostom's predecessor. A modern biographer of Chrysostom describes this development in these words:

Highly educated, and well grounded in the Scriptures, she had placed her services at the disposal of Archbishop Nektarios. The

---

[7]From the introduction to his translation of five of Chrysostom's letters to Olympia (NPNF¹ 9:287).
[8]Ibid.

courtly old man so valued her charitable generosity, and found her advice on church affairs so helpful, that he ordained her a deaconess when she was still in her early thirties, notwithstanding the ban imposed by St Paul [1 Tim 5.9], and quite recently reaffirmed by Emperor Theodosius, on consecrating widows under the age of sixty.[9]

Deaconesses were always more numerous and prominent in the eastern than in the western Church in the early centuries of Christianity. They were ordained in a formal way, as is evident from the service for the ordination of a deaconess that appears in the *Apostolic Constitutions*, a collection of ecclesiastical texts that dates from the second half of the fourth century (which strongly reflect usages in Syria). It is unclear to what extent, if any, the deaconesses served liturgically on a daily and weekly basis. We do know that they anointed women when they were baptized, since in those days people were baptized naked.[10]

Chrysostomus Baur, a prominent biographer of Chrysostom, asserts this concerning the deaconesses in Chrysostom's time:

> For the service of women, ecclesiastical deaconesses were assigned. These were widows, or older single women, who were consecrated by the bishop, in a special ceremony involving the laying on of hands, and the donation of a stole or chalice for the liturgical service of the Church. It was their special duty to keep order among the women at divine service [i.e., at the Divine Liturgy]; they gave them the kiss of peace, and also had to admonish the women who did not live as they should. They helped with the training of the women catechumens, anointed

---

[9]Kelly, *Golden Mouth*, 113.

[10]A major reason the order of deaconess faded out after the early centuries of Christianity was that there came to be fewer and fewer adult baptisms as the faith spread. With nearly all of the population of the Roman Empire converted to Christianity by around the year 500, almost all the baptisms performed were of infants.

them at baptism, and also had the duty of bringing Holy Communion to sick women.[11]

To help us understand the reasons for having deaconesses at that time, it is important to remember that in those days men and women lived much more separate lives than they do today—as seen especially in the separate "women's quarters" in homes, and in the fact that the men and the women stood on opposite sides of the church during services.

All of this led Chrysostom to appreciate the importance of the office of deaconess in the life of the Church in his time. As he stated once, in preaching on 1 Timothy 3.11 ("The women likewise must be serious"):

> Some have thought that this is said of women generally, but it is not so, for why would he [i.e., St Paul] introduce anything about women in general to interfere with his subject [in this passage, the requirements for the offices of bishop and deacon]? He is speaking of those who hold the rank [*axiōma*] of deaconesses [*diakonias*]. . . .[12] [T]his order is greatly [*sphodra*] necessary [*anangkaion*] and useful and honorable in the Church.[13]

[11]Baur, *John Chrysostom and His Time*, vol. 1, 155. Taking the Eucharist to sick women as they lay in their private quarters would have been very unseemly for male deacons or for priests (who were all male).

[12]Others, including certain scholars, assert that Paul was referring to the wives of the deacons at this point.

[13]Homily 11 on 1 Timothy, PG 62, 553D (NPNF[1] 13:441). Three of his other letters written from exile (Letters 94, 104, and 105) were addressed to another deaconess, named Pentadia, to whom he writes appreciatively. In Letter 6.1.D to Olympia, he speaks of the deaconess Sabiniana in these terms: "My lady Sabiniana the deaconess arrived here on the very same day that I arrived. She was burning and exhausted, for she is at the age that traveling is difficult. But with youthful zeal she declared that she felt none of the pain. And she said that she was ready to go to Scythia, since she had heard that we were to be taken there. She is ready, she said, never to leave us, but to be with us wherever we are."

A description of St Olympia's truly remarkable Christian lifestyle is given in *The Life of Olympia*:

> She lived faultlessly [*anendeōs*] in unmeasured tears night and day, "submitting to every ordinance of man for the sake of the Lord" (1 Pet 2.13), full of every reverence, bowing before the saints, venerating the bishops, honoring the presbyters, respecting the priests, welcoming the ascetics, being anxious for the virgins, supplying the widows, raising the orphans, shielding the elderly, looking after the weak, having compassion on sinners, guiding the lost, having pity on all, attending with all her heart to the poor, catechizing many unbelieving women and making provision for all their material necessities of life. Thus, she left a reputation for goodness throughout her whole life which is ever to be remembered. Having called from slavery to freedom her myriad household servants, she proclaimed them to be of equal honor [*isotimon*] as her own nobility [*eugeneias*].[14]

Another passage from this anonymous *Life* tells of her importance in assisting Archbishop Nectarius and other leaders in the Church, as well as many others:

> And I know that this completely virtuous and divinely inspired Olympia provided also for the blessed Nectarius, the archbishop of Constantinople, who was completely persuaded by her even in the affairs of the Church; and for Amphilochius, bishop of Iconium; and Optimus, and Peter, and Gregory the brother of the holy Basil; and Epiphanius the archbishop of Constantia in Cyprus; and many others of the saints and inspired fathers who lived in the capital city.
>
> Why is it necessary to say that she also bestowed upon them property in the country, and money? And when the aforesaid Optimus died in Constantinople at this time, she shut the eyes

[14] *The Life of Olympias*, 15 (SC 13 [2nd ed.], 440; Clark, 139).

of the great man with her own hands. In addition, she relieved the poor without measure in all ways. She sustained Antiochus of Ptolemais; and Acacius, the bishop of Beroea; and the holy Severian, the bishop of Gabala; and in a word, all the priests residing there, in addition to innumerable ascetics and virgins.[15]

Thus, it is not at all surprising that Deaconess Olympia quickly discovered she had much in common with the newly consecrated Archbishop John, once he took up residence in his living quarters at the Great Church in Constantinople early in 398. Both were deeply devoted to spirituality, almsgiving, asceticism, and the Scriptures.

She must have very quickly asked him to be her spiritual father (he was about thirteen years older than her), and to be a spiritual guide for the nuns under her. And he must have quickly embraced her as a spiritual daughter after his own heart. Besides all the other reasons he had for appreciating her, he greatly admired her for the way she resisted the strong pressure to remarry after becoming a very young widow, and instead dedicated the rest of her life and her wealth to the service of the Church. In this, she reminded him of his own mother, Anthusa, who also was widowed at a young age and never remarried.

In summarizing the relationship between St John and St Olympia, J. N. D. Kelly says, in his biography of Chrysostom:

> There was no one in Constantinople with whom he was to have a deeper or more sympathetic understanding, no one with whom he was to feel more at ease or to whom he was to pour out his heart more unreservedly.[16]

Olympia served Archbishop John his meals, trying to make sure that he ate enough wholesome food. Care had to be taken that his food would not overly tax his weak digestive system, which he had

---

[15]*The Life of Olympias*, 14 (SC 13 [2nd ed.], 436, 438; Clark, 138).
[16]Kelly, *Golden Mouth*, 113.

injured during his days of severe asceticism as a young monastic living in the caves near the city of Antioch in the 370s. Later, when St John was uncanonically deposed at the infamous Synod of the Oak in September of 403 in Constantinople, one of the many charges brought against him was that he ate alone with women. It is also true that he did not host lavish banquets for the clergy as his predecessor Nectarius had done, which was missed by more worldly members of the clergy.

After the Synod of the Oak, which was engineered by Archbishop Theophilus of Alexandria, with the strong support of Empress Eudoxia, who had turned against him, John was sent into exile. But he was brought back after only a few days, at the empress's urgent request—for there had been an ominous "shaking" in the imperial bedroom, due either to an earthquake, or perhaps a miscarriage. However, during the following months, many forces continued to work against him—especially on the part of those clergy who resented his personal austerity and his pressure on them to serve the Lord and his Church more diligently, and with less ostentation.

A decisive moment came when the Empress Eudoxia had a silver statue of herself set up opposite the entrance of the Great Church. Soon after, at a feastday for St John the Baptist, Archbishop John exclaimed, "Again Herodias dances, again she calls for the head of John."[17] This seemed to seal her animosity against him, setting the stage for her decision to send him into exile again in June of 404—an exile from which he would not return.

Even though John begged his followers never to start a schism in the Church on his account, many of his followers could not bear the injustice that he had endured for many months, culminating in his permanent exile. They felt that they could not accept the authority of those who had driven out their beloved teacher and spiritual guide, and had usurped his place in the Church.

[17]Cf. Mt 14.6–8.

Because of their opposition to the new leadership in the Church (especially the new Archbishop Arsacius), these followers of Chrysostom, called "Johnites," were slandered and persecuted in various ways, including his closest friend and confidante, the faithful Deaconess Olympia. As reported by Sozomen, an important Church historian of the fifth century, a Johnite priest named Tigrius "was stripped of his clothes, scourged on the back, bound hand and foot, and stretched on the rack."[18]

In the months after John was taken into exile, Olympia was twice put on trial on the preposterous charge of having started the fire that broke out and destroyed the cathedral when John was taken and led off into exile. Each time she was released after her spirited defense: "My past life ought to avert all suspicion from me, for I have devoted my large inheritance to the restoration of the temples of God."[19]

Olympia was also pressured by the imperial authorities to accept the new Archbishop Arsacius and enter into communion with him, but she adamantly refused. According to Sozomen,

> As the accusation against her [about the fire] was wholly unsubstantiated by proofs, and as the prefect found that he had no grounds on which he could justly blame her, he changed to a milder charge, as if desirous of advising her, finding fault with her and the other women because they refused communion with his bishop, although [he said] it was possible for them to repent and to change their own circumstances. They all, through fear, deferred to the advice of the prefect; but Olympia said to him, "It is not just that, after having been publicly calumniated, without having had anything proved against me in the courts, I should be obliged to clear myself of charges totally unconnected with the accusation in question. . . . For even if you resort to unlawful compulsion, I will not hold communion with those from whom

---

[18]Sozomen, *Ecclesiastical History* 8.24 (NPNF[2] 2:415).
[19]Cf. Sozomen, *Ecclesiastical History* 8.24 (NPNF[2] 2:415). He also says that she defended herself with "great fortitude" (NPNF[2] 2:414).

I ought to secede, nor consent to anything that is not lawful to the pious." The prefect, finding that he could not prevail upon her to hold communion with Arsacius, dismissed her.[20]

As Olympia underwent these trials, and as John was being taken into exile by imperial guards (on a four-hundred-mile journey eastward to Cucusus), he wrote to her immediately to assure her of his well-being, to inquire after her health and welfare, and most especially, to help her emerge from and stay out of the grip of despondency. For her part, due to the persecution of the Johnites by the ecclesiastical and civil authorities, her physical welfare was very much in danger. But her worst affliction after John was sent off into exile was indeed her tendency to fall into despondency and even despair, so difficult it was for her to accept what had happened to her beloved spiritual father, as well as all the ensuing persecution—some of which came from the hands of those whom she had previously supported—such as Bishop Acacius of Berea and Bishop Antiochus of Ptolemais.

Some time in the following year (405), Olympia left the capital in a kind of self-imposed exile, and settled in Nicomedia, in western Asia Minor, where she continued her life of charitable works. Before she left the capital, she carefully entrusted the care and supervision of the nuns in her monastery to her kinswoman and spiritual daughter, Marina.

Two years later, Chrysostom died at Comana on a forced march to a place of further exile in northeastern Asia Minor, on September 14, 407. Olympia reposed in the Lord in the following year, on July 25, 408, in Nicomedia. Hence she is commemorated in the Orthodox Church on July 25.

The Life of Olympia[21] was written by an anonymous author within a few decades of her death. She is also mentioned by Sozomen[22] and by Bishop Palladius in his *Lausiac History* (2.56). She is

[20]Ibid. (NPNF[2] 2:415).
[21]See above (footnote 2).
[22]Sozomen, *Ecclesiastical History* 8.9.24, 27.

discussed at greater length by this same Palladius in his *Dialogue on the Life of St John Chrysostom.*[23]

Another *Life* of Olympia was written by a later abbess of her monastery, named Sergia, in the seventh century.[24] Abbess Sergia's account records various miracles that occurred when St Olympia's relics were transferred, at her direction, from a monastery outside Constantinople to the monastery that Olympia had founded, which adjoined the Great Church of the capital city. In her account, Sergia states simply, "I report this: that the holy, precious remains of this pious and virtuous Olympias have cured many people, both men and women, from impure demons and other diseases."[25] Later, in the fourteenth century, the Byzantine historian Nicephoras Callistus wrote of her in his *Ecclesiastical History* (13.24).

The Letters

Seventeen letters have come down to us that were written by St John Chrysostom to St Olympia during his exile. These are only a small portion of all his extant letters—some 236 of them, written to about 150 different people while he was in exile. Of all these letters, the great patrologist Johannes Quasten declares, "The longest and most cordial are the seventeen communications which he wrote to the widow and deaconess Olympias."[26]

The letters are remarkable in a number of ways—perhaps most especially for the insights they provide into the personal lives and feelings of two illustrious saints, and some of the dynamics of their relationship. The sheer beauty of his writing is a joy to experience, as these letters are all suffused with the same grand eloquence that

[23]See above (footnote 2).

[24]This *Life*, called "Sergia's Narration," is given in English translation in *Jerome, Chrysostom, and Friends*, Elizabeth Clark, ed., 145–57.

[25]"Sergia's Narration" (Clark, 150–51).

[26]Johannes Quasten, *Patrology: Volume III—The Golden Age of Greek Patristic Literature* (Westminster, MD: Christian Classics, Inc., 1986 [1st ed. 1950]), 469.

characterizes all his preaching and writing. Certainly this is indicative of his very high esteem for her—although he may have also surmised that they would be read by others at the time and in the future.

Unfortunately, none of her letters to him have come down to us. But in some of his letters to her he refers to her letters, in which she expressed alternating moods of cheerfulness and discouragement or despondency (*athymia*)—sometimes, apparently, even deep despondency. This inspired Chrysostom to address the spiritual battle with despondency from many angles in his letters. Indeed, the most common theme in these letters is that of instructing Olympia how to avert and overcome the despondency that continually plagues her. It is fascinating to watch St John as he seems to try everything he can think of to help lift Olympia's spirits.

In the letters Chrysostom repeatedly expresses his conviction that despondency is brought on and sustained by *faulty thinking*—by negative, debilitating *thoughts* (*logismoi*)—and so he is likewise convinced that it can be willfully overcome through *proper thinking*.[27] Thus he spends much time in the letters trying to encourage, inspire, empower, and convince Olympia to focus on healthful, life-giving thoughts—including thoughts about the future spiritual rewards that she is surely accumulating for herself through her valiant endurance of all the calamities that both she and he are suffering.[28]

---

[27]This is not to suggest that Chrysostom would be opposed to any other means that might be helpful in the treatment of despondency or depression. He himself made use of medicine for his frequent stomach ailments, as we see in Letter 17, where he thanks "my lady the most decorous Synkletia" for sending him a certain very effective medicine.

[28]This emphasis on proper thinking as the key to getting out of—and staying out of—despondency/despair/depression is the hallmark of the widespread clinical approach in modern psychotherapy known as Cognitive Behavioral Therapy (CBT). A classic work in this field is Michael Edelstein, *Three Minute Therapy: Change Your Thinking, Change Your Life* (Aurora, CO: Glenbridge Publications, 1997). The affinity of some basic aspects of this approach with sound Orthodox spirituality can be seen, for instance, in the teachings of the renowned Serbian elder, Thaddeus of Vitovnica, in the book *Our Thoughts Determine Our Lives: The Life and Teachings of Elder Thaddeus of Vitovnica* (Platina, CA: St. Herman of Alaska Brotherhood, 2009), as well as in the

In all of this, St John often reminds Olympia that this world, with all its misery, is passing away, that what we suffer temporarily in this world—if we do so patiently, without complaining, and with thanksgiving—is producing for us great spiritual rewards in the next life, that the greater the struggle, the greater the gain, even in this life, and that her enemies, through the slanders and other forms of persecution to which they are subjecting her, are actually making it possible for her to gain greater crowns—though again, this depends on her enduring the hardships nobly.

These are all themes that resound throughout all of St John's writings—indeed, bearing suffering nobly is probably the most common theme in his entire corpus. And how appropriate it seems that the Lord asked him to put his words into action in such a dramatic, intense way during the last three years of his life—when he was given such an extended opportunity to endure graciously his unjust deposition and exile, as well as the physical ravages he endured during the years of exile that ended with his death, at the age of only fifty-eight. His victory in this lengthy and difficult struggle is evident in his famous last words: "Glory to God for all things." It is noteworthy that in Letter 4 to Olympia, he writes, "Glory to God for all things—and I have not ceased repeating these words in the midst of everything that is happening to me."[29]

Interestingly, in some of his letters to her, he also urges her to reflect often upon her past deeds of virtue—especially her vast amount of almsgiving through the offering of her immense fortune to the Church and its social work—in order to raise her spirits. He seems to have no fear that doing so might tempt her to be overly

teachings of many other Orthodox spiritual directors. For more on the affinity, as well as the key differences, between traditional Orthodox spiritual direction and Cognitive Behavioral Therapy, see the excellent work by the Athonite Monk, Fr Alexis (Trader), *Ancient Christian Wisdom and Aaron Beck's Cognitive Therapy: A Meeting of Minds* (New York, NY: Peter Lang Publishing, 2011). For an example of a specific, detailed, patristically-centered analysis of despondency, see Gabriel Bunge, *Despondency: The Spiritual Teaching of Evagrius Ponticus on Acedia* (Crestwood, NY: St Vladimir's Seminary Press, 2012).

[29]Letter 4.1.b.

proud of her accomplishments in a spiritually damaging way. Here we see him putting into action the traditional Orthodox pastoral practice of adjusting the spiritual medicine to the unique disposition and circumstances of each patient.[30]

Chrysostom is also particularly emphatic about the role that Olympia's free-will must play in her deliverance from the throes of despondency. In all his writings, he often speaks of the crucial importance of exerting our free-will to resist evil and do the good—to *cooperate* with divine grace in the process of developing virtues and ultimately gaining eternal salvation. So in these letters it is not surprising that he expresses great confidence in her ability to exert her free-will to "throw off this heavy burden of despondency [*athymia*],"[31] to "be far removed from despondency."[32] He directly exhorts her: "stop torturing yourself,"[33] and "drive away the despondency that now envelopes you, and do not inflict exaggerated and grievous punishments on yourself."[34]

St John appeals to the power of her will to drive away despondency knowing full well how grievous this affliction can be. As he says in Letter 10:

Despondency [*athymia*] is for souls a grievous torture chamber, unspeakably painful, more fierce and bitter than every ferocity and torment. It imitates the poisonous worm that attacks not only the body but also the soul, and not only the bones but also the mind. It is a continual executioner who not only tears in pieces one's torso but also mutilates the strength of one's soul. (Letter 10.2.b)

[30]For a brilliant, brief exposition of this very flexible approach to the care of souls, see Canon 102 of the Quinisext Council of 692 (the second half of the Sixth Ecumenical Council) (NPNF[2] 14:408).

[31]Letter 5.1.c.

[32]Letter 10.14.f.

[33]Letter 14.1.a.

[34]Letter 17.4.b.

Nevertheless, as powerful as despondency can be, he is convinced that she can overcome it, through the power of her own will, working in cooperation with God's grace—and inspired by his ardent desire and will for her to be free from this affliction. As he says to her in Letter 8,

> Therefore, if you wish to fill us with great joyfulness—which I know you wish for, and have zealously pursued—show us that you have completely chased away the burden of despondency, and that you are filled with calm. (Letter 8.13.c)

And of course, as with everything in the spiritual life, prayer is a great key. As he reminds her in Letter 7, "ceaselessly beseech God" for his help in the struggle.

The letters are also highlighted by very remarkable, lengthy discourses on the patient endurance of several biblical figures. St John writes of Job's valiant, uncomplaining endurance of suffering (Job is St John's favorite figure from the Old Testament, whom he calls "that great athlete of patience"[35]). He writes of Lazarus, who sat at the rich man's gate, and gained salvation through uncomplainingly enduring his wretched physical state and being constantly spurned by the rich man,[36] and of Joseph, the patriarch Jacob's son, whose valiant resistance to the sinful overtures of his master's wife, and his uncomplaining acceptance of his completely unjust imprisonment in Egypt, leave St John in wonder.[37] Finally, he points to St Paul, who learns through his own great trials and tribulations that indeed the Lord's strength is made perfect in weakness.[38] St John brings all of these vivid examples before Olympia to inspire her, to stir her, to rouse her to refuse to be dejected in the midst of all her own troubles and afflictions—and rather to accept them calmly and graciously.

[35]Letter 10.6.b and 17.2.b, cf. 14.1.c.
[36]Letter 10.8.b, cf. Lk 16.19–31.
[37]Letter 10.10.c–14.d.
[38]Letter 10.9.e, cf. 2 Cor 12.9.

In addition, the letters are tinged with the poignant possibility that John and Olympia will never see each other again in this life. Yet he continued to hope that some day they would be reunited, and he also urged her to have this same hope. He says in Letter 8 that he knows she is yearning to see him again,

> which causes you to weep continually and to say to everyone, "We no longer hear that voice of his, we no longer enjoy his teaching that we were so accustomed to. We are tortured by hunger. For that which God threatened to bring upon the Hebrews long ago, now we are enduring—'not a famine of bread, neither of water, but a famine of divine instruction.'" (Letter 8.11.a, cf. Am 8.11)

He then says touchingly,

> What, therefore, shall we say about these things? That certainly it is possible for you, in my absence, to have fellowship with me through my books. And we will make haste, if we can locate couriers, to send you numerous, long letters. But if you desire to hear my living voice, perhaps this is possible, and we will see each other again, God willing—or rather, not "perhaps," but surely, without a doubt! For now, I will remind you that I have not said these things rashly—neither have I beguiled you, nor made a miscalculation—but that you may hear my living voice through my letters. (Letter 8.11.b)

Similarly, he ends Letter 13 with a strong exhortation: "And by no means ever give up hope that we will see each other again." And near the end of his last letter to her, he writes, very movingly:

> If it is being separated from us that causes your despondency, expect to be freed from this. And I don't say this now just to comfort you, but because I know that this surely will happen. If

it were not meant to be, I think I should long ago have been set free from this life here below, considering the trials that have been inflicted upon me. (Letter 17.4.a)

Another important aspect of their relationship is revealed clearly in Letter 9. This is the fact that St John trusted Olympia, more than any of his other supporters in Constantinople, to help him continue his attempts to direct certain affairs of the Church, even while he is in exile. This also is poignant, considering that he will never return to the capital until his relics are brought back in triumph thirty-one years after his death. And it is dramatic, since all this must be done with utmost secrecy, for they knew that their many enemies were eager to intercept their letters, seeking to thwart their efforts to guide the Church, and looking for more ways to slander them.

Letter 9 is also intriguing because in it St John gives a lengthy, detailed account of what he had to endure in the city of Caesarea in Cappadocia, on the way to his place of exile in Cucusus. He vividly describes how he barely managed to survive attacks by marauding Isaurians, and terrible sickness, including dangerously high fevers, as well as the machinations and threats of his enemies within the Church, including the local bishop, Pharetrius.

Letter 12 is particularly interesting in that he openly recounts the severe difficulties he suffered from sickness during his first winter in Cucusus:

I spent these past two months no better than dead—yea, even worse than dead. I was surviving just enough to perceive the terrible things encircling me everywhere. All was night to me—the day, the dawn, the height of noonday—and I spent the whole time nailed to my bed. I tried a myriad of ways to alleviate the wound caused by the cold, but they all failed. When I kindled a fire, I had to endure the most grievous smoke; and when I enclosed myself in one little room, having a myriad of blankets, and not daring to set foot over the threshold, I suffered the

most extreme torments—continual vomiting, headaches, lack
of appetite, and constant sleeplessness. I spent the whole time
as if it were a vast sea of night. (Letter 12.1.a)

His complete candor in this description is noteworthy; though, perhaps with a wry smile, he opens this letter with these words:

It is after having mounted up from the very gates of death that
I am writing to Your Moderation [*kosmiotēta*]. Therefore I am
rejoicing greatly that your servants have come to see us now,
while we are "anchored in port." For if they had arrived while
I was still being tossed on the sea, suffering from the dreadful waves of my illness, it would not have been easy for me to
deceive Your Piety through sending you good news instead of
bad.

Altogether, these letters are a glowing testimony of love in action
on the part of one of our most famous and beloved saints toward a
tender-hearted, long-suffering sister in Christ, his spiritual daughter
Olympia, whose saintliness—especially her courage in the midst of
intense heartache and struggle—also shines through these letters,
helping us to understand why she also is honored as an illustrious
saint in her own right.

May these letters bring all of us into closer communion with
these remarkable saints.

Manuscripts of the Letters

These seventeen letters appear in Greek and Latin in volume 52
(col. 549–623) of J.-P. Migne's classic series, the *Patrologia Graeca*,
published in Paris from 1857 to 1866. They also appear in Greek and
French in volume 13 in the *Sources chrétiennes* series, also published
in Paris, in 1947 and again in 1968, by Les Editions du Cerf. Both SC

editions were edited and translated by Anne-Marie Malingrey. In the second edition Malingrey produced a critical Greek text of the letters and slightly revised her translation. I based my translation on the Greek text given in SC 13 (2nd ed.), in consultation with the French translation. I follow the SC text divisions, and the PG column numbers are noted in the margins.

For five of the letters to Olympia (Letters 7, 9, 12, 16, and 17), after doing the basic translation from the Greek, I consulted an older English translation (done by W. R. W. Stephens in 1889) that appears in the *Nicene and Post-Nicene Fathers* set (NPNF[1] 9:289–304). Interestingly, the five letters given there are not presented in chronological order (nor do they follow the PG ordering).[39]

Apparently the other twelve letters to Olympia have never appeared in English translation before now.

A Note on Names in the Translation

Since this is a translation from Greek into English, I have chosen to use, for the most part, the most common English forms of the names that appear in the text. This is why I have called the deaconess *Olympia* instead of *Olympias* (*Olympiada* is another form of the same Greek name).

[39]The SC and PG order differ for all but one letter (the NPNF follows yet another order):

SC	PG	NPNF	SC	PG	NPNF
1	11		10	3	
2	10		11	5	
3	9		12	6	3
4	12		13	7	
5	8		14	16	
6	13		15	15	
7	1	1	16	17	5
8	2		17	4	2
9	14	4			

Very shortly after the beginning of his journey into exile

June, 404[1]

To my Lady, the deaconess Olympia, most venerable and most beloved by God, from John the bishop, greetings in the Lord.

1.A However much we are stretched by our trials, by so much do [609] our consolations increase, giving us firmer hopes for the future. For now everything is flowing along well for us, and we are sailing with fair winds. Who could have foreseen this? Who could have foretold? Reefs and shoals, whirlpools and hurricanes all threaten shipwreck—a moonless night, darkest gloom, precipices and crags. And yet through all this we are settled, sailing on such seas that we are no worse off than a ship rocking in a harbor.

B Taking all these things into account, therefore, my lady most beloved by God, be lifted up above these tumults and billowing waves, and deem me worthy to make known to me everything concerning your health. For our part, we are in good health and joyful spirits. Indeed, my body has become stronger, as we are breathing pure air. And the guards who are conducting us into exile are taking such good care of us that we have no need of servants, for they are carrying out those tasks. And they have taken upon themselves this

---

[1]The dates given at the beginning of each letter do not appear in the original manuscripts.

office out of their great love for us. And among all the bodyguards, each one esteems himself blessed through this service.

c   There is only one thing that causes us pain—not being assured that you also are in good spirits. Let me know this, so that we may rejoice with great joy, and so that we may render many thanks to my lord and your mostly greatly longed for [spiritual] child, Pergamius. For if you desire to write to us, make use of him for this—since he is trustworthy, he is strongly attached to us, and he is full of respect for your propriety and your piety.

From Nicaea, after one month
on his journey into exile

July 3, 404

1.A And now to deliver you from any alarm about our journey: as [608]
I wrote to you recently, my body has been prospering in health and
greater strength. For the air is benefiting us beautifully, and those
who are guarding us are tending to our needs with great zeal, taking
great care to offer us relief. We are about to leave Nicaea as I send
you this letter, on the third day of the month of July.

B Write us frequently about your health. My lord Pergamius, in
whom I have great trust, will serve you in this. Do not only inform
me about your health, but also about whether you have scattered
the cloud of your despondency [*athymias*]. And if we learn of this
through letters from you, then we will send you letters even more
often, since we will have obtained a better result through writing to
you. Moreover, if you wish to enjoy a greater frequency of letters
from me, show me clearly that something better results from such
frequency, and you will see that you will be having letters in abundance.

C However, for now, since many people have come from there [609]
[i.e., from Constantinople] who could have brought me letters from
you, not having received a letter from Your Excellency has caused
me great pain.

33

After two months on his journey into exile, upon nearing Caesarea of Cappadocia in Asia Minor

End of July, 404

1.A When I see these crowds of men and women on the roads, in [608] the hostels, and in the towns streaming forth to see us, and seeing them weeping, I wonder about what thoughts and feelings you are having. For if these people whom we have seen are weeping so profusely because of their despondency, such that they cannot be easily consoled, but rather when I pray and supplicate and exhort them to stop, they burst out with floods of even hotter tears, it is manifest that for you the tempest is still more violent. But however more violent the tempest is, greater still are the prizes in the contest, if you endure it with thanksgiving and with manly courage,[1] which is exactly the appropriate way for you to bear it. For when a wind blows fiercely, if the pilots deploy the sails skillfully, they keep the boat under control; and if they steer it carefully, in the proper way, they sail with great security.

B Knowing these things, therefore, my lady most beloved by God, do not give yourself over to the tyranny of despair, but conquer the

---

[1]"Manly courage" may sound jarring to modern ears, especially in reference to a woman, but Chrysostom obviously used it with confidence that Olympia would not be offended by it. Further, since Chrysostom expects Olympia to be able to have "manly courage," it does not imply that this quality can only be possessed by men. The Greek word for courage (*andreia*) comes from the word for man (*anēr*).

storm with reason [*tō logismō*]. You can do it, for the surging sea is not stronger than your ability to master it. Send me letters proclaiming this to me, so that, while enduring being in a foreign land, we may rejoice with great joy, knowing that with the understanding [*syneseōs*] and wisdom [*philosophia*][2] that befit you, you have borne this despondency well.

I have written these things to you, Your Excellency, while drawing near to Caesarea.

---

[2]Chrysostom consistently uses this word in reference to the Christian way of life and thought, with the conviction that Christianity is the highest form and the summit of all philosophy.

From Caesarea of Cappadocia, after about two months on his journey into exile

August, 404

I.A Having survived the illness that afflicted me on the way, because [609] of which I took rest at Caesarea, and having now been restored to perfect health, I am writing to you circumspectly[1] from Caesarea—this city in which I have enjoyed great solicitude, having encountered some excellent, extremely reputable doctors who succeeded in their healing ministry to me not only through their skill but also by their sympathy and love. One of them even offered to accompany us on our journey, even though there are already many people traveling with us.

B I am often writing to you about the things concerning us; however, even though I have previously reproached you about this, you are rarely writing to me. And you should know that this is due to your negligence—for there is no lack of people who could bring me letters from you. For instance, my lord, the brother of the blessed Maximus the bishop, came two days ago; and when we asked him for letters, he said that no one had entrusted any to him. And when we asked the priest Tigrius the same thing, we got the same response.

---

[1]St John feels he must be careful in his letter-writing because of all his enemies who would take delight in intercepting one of his letters.

So I beseech you, reproach him about this—our sincere, warm, and beloved friend—and the others who are all in the company of [610] Kyriakos the bishop. On account of the change of our residence, do not trouble them or anyone else about this. We have received grace. Perhaps they wanted to help, but were unable to do so. Glory to God for all things—and I have not ceased repeating these words in the midst of everything that is happening to me.[2] Be it so, that they were not able to help. But were they not able at least to write?

c   Give many thanks to my ladies, the sisters of my lord the most honorable Bishop Pergamius, who have been very helpful on our behalf. They have rendered his son-in-law, my lord the governor, so well disposed toward us that he himself greatly desires for us to stay there.

As for you, frequently give us news of your health and of those whom we love. Be without a care for us, for we are in good health and joy, and we are enjoying a great respite even until this very day.

d   I desire to learn whether my friends with Bishop Kyriakos have been set free, since no one has said anything to me clearly about this. Try to make this known to us. And tell Bishop Kyriakos that if I do not write to him, it is due to my pain.

[2] As is quite well known, St John's last words before his death were "Glory to God for all things."

A little after the previous letter, after leaving Caesarea

August, 404

1.A Having left the city [Caesarea], it was not likely for us to have [607] been set free from those people who are trying to crush our spirit. Nevertheless, those who met us on the way—whether they were from the East, or from Armenia, or from anywhere else on the earth—gushed forth fountains of tears upon seeing us, along with wailing; and the entire journey is being accompanied by these lamentations.

I'm telling you these things so you may know that I have many fellow-sufferers with us, and this is not a small source of consolation. How unbearably oppressive the opposite would be—as the prophet explains, saying, "I waited for someone who would suffer along with me, but there was no one; I looked for those who would comfort me, but I found none."[1]

It is manifest that I am provided with a tremendous consolation, having the whole world sharing in my distress. And if you are looking for another consolation, we, who have suffered evils so great and so numerous, are abiding in health, in freedom from fear, in great inner stillness [*hēsychia*]. And in reckoning up our incessant, multiple sufferings, the tribulations, the treacherous plots against us, I am ceaselessly reveling [*entryphontes*] in the memory of all these things.

---

[1] Ps 69.20 (68.21, LXX).

B   Therefore, you yourself, in reflecting upon these things, scatter the cloud of despondency and write to us continually about your health. Now that my most beloved lord Arabius has come bringing me messages, I am astounded that Your Excellency has not sent me anything, even though my noble lady, married to him, is exceedingly dear to me.

Consider this: that the pleasant and sorrowful things of this present life are altogether passing away. If the gate is narrow and the way is hemmed in, still it is a way. Remember the word that I have often given you: if the gate is wide and the way is broad, it is also a way. And now, escaping from the earth, and especially from the bond of the flesh, open the wings of your wisdom [*philosophia*], not letting it be submerged by shadows and smoke—that is, by human affairs— nor drawn down earthward. And if you behold those who have caused us such great evil still having their cities and their power, enjoying honor—and having bodyguards!—repeat these words: "Wide is the gate and broad is the way leading to destruction";[2] and because of this, weep for them, and groan. For the one doing evil here, and yet not suffering punishment, and enjoying honor from men, will suffer greater retribution having such honor. This is why that rich man is burning bitterly, not only because of the cruelty he showed to Laza-
[608] rus, but also because in the prosperity that he enjoyed continually in the midst of such cruelty, he did not become better.[3]

C   Meditating upon these things within yourself, and similar things—for we have not stopped chanting such things continually to you—my lady most beloved by God, throw off this heavy burden of despondency. Make it evident to us, as I have written to you previously, that our letters are a great source of comfort to you; for knowing that, I will provide this remedy more often.

[2]Mt 7.13.
[3]Cf. Lk 16.19–32.

From Cucusus, after
three months in exile

Late September, 404

1.A We could scarcely breathe when we arrived in Cucusus—from [610] here we are now writing to you. And we could scarcely see clearly on account of the smoke and the variegated cloud of evils that befell us on the way. Now, since these afflictions have passed, we are recounting them to Your Piety.

When we were in the midst of them, I did not wish to write to you about them, lest I make you greatly sorrowful. For nearly thirty full days I did not cease fighting with most grievous fevers; and while making the long and painful journey we were assailed by various, most severe stomach disorders. Think of my predicament: besides being without doctors, or baths, or daily necessities, or any other respite, we were assailed on all sides by fear of the Isaurians,[1] and by other evils that one customarily has to bear when traveling—anxious concern, disquietude, and the absence of those who could care for us. But now all these things have passed.

B Having come to Cucusus, we are entirely freed from the malady, along with its consequences, and we are in perfect health. We have been delivered from the fear of the Isaurians, since many soldiers are here, who are heavily armed against them. The necessities of life are

---

[1]The Isaurians were a tribe residing in eastern Asia Minor that frequently sent out marauding bands into the surrounding regions.

everywhere readily available to us; and we have been received with every kindness.

[611]   And although the countryside is most desolate, my lord Dioscorus happened to be here. He's the one who sent me a servant while I was in Caesarea, expressly to beg and supplicate me not to prefer someone else's house over his, since many others had offered the same. I considered it needful to select his house over the others, so I went to his. And now he is everything for us, so much so that I continually protest to him because of his profuse liberality and the abundance that he wishes to bestow upon us. Indeed, on our account he moved to this country, in order to serve us by every means. So he is now preparing a house for us to stay in for the winter, making sure that everything necessary is being provided. In a word, he is overlooking nothing in his service to us. And many other stewards and household managers, having been commanded by their own masters through letters, are continually arriving, ready to do everything to give us relief and comfort.

c   I have told you all this—on the one hand, the things that I suffered in the past; and on the other hand, I've told you the good things—so that no one will hastily suppose that we are about to rise up from here. If those who wish to do us a favor would allow us to reside where we wish, and if they would not again assign us to a place of their own choosing, I would indeed accept it as a favor. But if they are about to make us leave here, and transfer us to another place, which would mean another journey and another exile, this would be exceedingly more grievous to me. At first we feared being sent to a more remote and more wretched country, but now just undertaking another journey would be worse to me than ten thousand exiles. For it was the difficulty of being moved a far distance that brought us even to the doors of death.

Now we are staying in Cucusus, renewing our strength by remaining in one place, and recovering from the great fatigue that we've had for so long. And thanks to the rest, we are tending to our burning bones and exhausted flesh.

D My lady Sabiniana the deaconess arrived here on the very same day that I arrived. She was burning and exhausted, for she is at the age that traveling is difficult. But with youthful zeal she declared that she felt none of the pain. And she said that she was ready to go to Scythia, since she had heard that we were to be taken there. She is ready, she said, never to leave us, but to be with us wherever we are.

The people of the Church have been tremendously welcoming, with great zeal and solicitude. My lord Constantine,[2] the most pious priest, has been here for some time. He had written to me, pleading that I would permit to him to come here, since he would not have dared to come without my counsel. He especially desired to come, he said, since it was not possible for him to remain where he was; for as he tells me, he is constrained by evil circumstances to conceal and hide himself.

E Now I supplicate you not to exert your influence any longer concerning the place of my residence. However, if you find out that [612] they are thinking more about this, say nothing about it; but with your customary finesse, ascertain where they are intending to send me. You can do it. If you find out that it is nearby here, or in a town by the sea, perhaps in Cyzicus or near Nicomedia,[3] accept it. But if it is far from the place I'm now in, or even further away, do not accept that. For that would be terribly difficult and most grievous for me.

For the present we are enjoying here a great respite, such that in two days, every trace of the unpleasantness that happened to me during the journey disappeared.

---

[2]Sabiniana and Constantine were both from Antioch, St John's hometown.

[3]These two cities were located much closer to Constantinople, in western Asia Minor.

From Cucusus, after about six months in exile

Late 404

1.A Come now, let us again alleviate the wound of your despondency, and scatter the thoughts [*logismous*] that gather around you like a cloud. What is it that upsets your mind? Is it because of the wild storm which has come upon the churches, enveloping all things in darkness like a moonless night, and coming to a head each day, travailing to cause cruel shipwrecks, and increasing the ruination of the world? I myself know this also, and no one can contradict it. [549]

If you wish, I will depict an image of what has happened, to make the tragedy more vivid to you.

I behold a sea in fury everywhere, forced open to the depths of the abyss, revealing corpses floating on the waves, others submerged beneath them; the bridges of the ships destroyed, the sails in shreds, the masts shattered, the oars fallen out of the hands of the oarsmen; the pilots seated upon the decks in front of the tillers, with their hands crossed over their knees, and in the face of their impotence before these events, they are groaning, crying out in anguish, lamenting, wailing; with nothing clearly visible, neither the sky nor the sea, but with everything plunged into deep darkness, with such obscurity and gloom that upon turning around it's impossible to recognize one's neighbor; and with the sailors everywhere beset by crashing waves, and by monsters of the sea.

But how long will we pursue that which is impossible to grasp? For whatever imagery I search for to portray the current evils, words are powerless to suffice.

B   However, even when I see such things, I do not give up an even firmer hope, as I consider the Pilot governing everything, who prevails over storms, who calms the raging gale, not through skill and artfulness, but with a single nod. It is not at their beginning—not immediately, when they first arise—that he customarily obliterates evils, but when they increase, when they come to their furthest point [*telos*], when most men fall into despair, then he does wondrous things beyond all expectation, demonstrating his own power, and training the patience of those who have fallen.

C   Therefore, do not be cast down, I beseech you. For there is only one thing, Olympia, to fear, only one real temptation, and that is sin. This is the refrain that I keep chanting to you ceaselessly. For everything else is ultimately a fable—whether you speak of plots, or enmities, or deceptions, or slanders, or abuses, or accusations, or confiscations, or banishments, or sharpened swords, or high seas, or war engulfing the entire world. Whichever of these you point to, they [550] are transitory and perishable, and they only affect mortal bodies; they cannot in any way injure the watchful soul. This is why, wishing to express the paltriness of both the good and the bad things of this present life, the blessed Paul stated the matter in one phrase, saying, "For the things that are seen are transient."[1]

So why are you fearing temporal things, which flow past like river streams? For this is the nature of present things, whether they be pleasant or painful. Another prophet compared all the happiness of mankind not to grass, but to something else even more ephemeral, when he pronounced everything in this life to be like the *flower* of the grass. He did not so describe just one portion of earthly affairs in this way—such as riches, or luxury, or power, or honors; but all the

---

[1] 2 Cor 4.18.

things that appear to men to be splendid he encompassed in a single word—*glory*—when he brought in the image of the grass in saying, "All the glory of man is like the flower of the grass."[2]

2.A Adversity is indeed terrible and miserable. But look at it again through another comparison, and despise it all the more. For slanders and insults and reproaches and mockeries on the part of enemies, and their evil plots, are compared to a worn out garment and moth-eaten wool when the Lord says through the same prophet, "Do not fear the reproaches of men, and do not be discomfited by their reviling; for like a garment they will be worn out, and like wool by the moth they will be devoured."[3]

B Therefore, do not let yourself be troubled by what's happening. And stop beseeching this or that person for help, and running after shadows—for this is what human assistance amounts to—and instead, ceaselessly beseech God, whom you serve, simply to give a nod; and in one moment [*mia kairou*] of time everything is brought into proper order. But if, in beseeching him for help, this does not come about quickly, this is how he often works—not crushing the evils immediately (to return to my previous line of reasoning), but when they come to a head, when they increase, when there remains almost nothing that has not been ravaged by the evils of the enemies, then all at once he changes everything to tranquillity, and leads things to an unexpected stability. For he is able to accomplish not only what we expect and hope for, but what is much more, and what is infinitely greater. Therefore Paul says, "to the one who is able to do more than everything, even exceedingly more than we can ask or think."[4]

[2] Is 11.6.
[3] Is 51.7–8.
[4] Eph 3.20.

C   Would it not have been possible for him, from the beginning, to have prevented the three youths from suffering their trial?[5] But [551] he did not wish to do that, so that they could amass great profit. For this reason he allowed them to be turned over into the hands of the barbarians, and the flames of the furnace to shoot up to an immeasurable height, and the wrath of the king to be enkindled more fearsomely than the furnace, and their hands and their feet to be tied extremely tightly, and they themselves to be thrown into the fire. And when all the onlookers gave up hope of their being rescued, then all at once, and beyond all hope, the mighty wonder-working power of God, the master Craftsman, appeared, shining forth with exceeding brilliance. For the fire became bound, and the bound ones were delivered, and the furnace became a temple of prayer, a fountain of dew more awesome than the courts of kings. And fire, radiantly blazing, more powerful than iron and stone, and holding mastery over every other substance, was conquered by the strands of their hair. And an all-harmonious choir stood on that very spot, as the holy ones summoned all of creation unto the marvelous melody. They sent up hymns of thanksgiving for having been bound and set on fire by their enemies, and for having been driven from their homeland, for having been made prisoners, for having been deprived of their freedom, for having been banished and made homeless wanderers, and for having to sojourn in a foreign and barbarous land—it was fitting for a prudent soul to be thankful for all of this.

D   For when the malicious schemes of their enemies reached their height (for what more could they do beyond putting the youths to death?), and the labors of the athletes were fulfilled, and their crowns were woven, and their rewards were prepared, and nothing remained to do to give them glory, then the evils were scattered, and the very one who had lit the furnace and had delivered them to such tortuous punishment [i.e., King Nebuchadnezzar] became

[5]Cf. Dan 3.

a wondrous panegyrist of those holy athletes and a herald of the marvelous wonderworking of God. He sent letters all over the earth filled with praises, recounting what had occurred, thus becoming a most faithful herald of the marvelous wonderworking of God.[6] So now the one who had been an enemy and an adversary is writing things that could not be doubted, even by enemies.

3.A Do you see the ingenious skillfulness of God? Do you see his wisdom? Do you see his paradoxical way of operating? Do you see his love for mankind, and his solicitude? Therefore, do not be dismayed, do not be shaken; but instead, continually give thanks to him for all things, glorifying him, calling upon him, beseeching him, and pleading with him.

And even if a myriad of fears, a myriad of tumults, assail you, and conflagrations, and whatever else are laid before your eyes, let none of them trouble you. For the Master is not outmatched by the difficulty of these things, even if everything is brought to the verge of destruction. For he is able to raise up those who have fallen, and to set aright those who have gone astray, and to correct those who have been ensnared, and to set free and make righteous those who have been filled with a multitude of sins, and to give life to those who are dead, and to render more brilliant those things which have been razed to the ground, and to make new those things which have grown old. For if he brings into being those things which had not [552] existed, and if he graces with existence those things which in no way had anywhere appeared before, then much more will he guide aright those things which already exist.

B But aren't there many who are dying, many who are scandalized? Yes, there are many, and such things have often happened. Yet afterwards all have received their appropriate correction, except for some who have remained incorrigible even after a change in their circumstances.

[6]Cf. Dan 4.1–3.

Why are you disquieted and distressed because one person is cast out and another is welcomed? Christ was crucified, and Barabbas, the thief, was set free, since the depraved crowd cried out to have the murderer saved, rather than their Savior and benefactor. How many, do you think, were scandalized then? How many perished during that time?

c   But it is needful for us to return to the higher topic at hand. This Man who was crucified—was he not from his birth an exile, a fugitive, and did he not have to flee with his whole family into exile in a foreign, barbarous land when he was scarcely out of his swaddling bands? And torrents of blood resulted from the event of Christ's flight [into Egypt], and cruel murders, and slaughters; and those of tender age, just as if they had been arrayed in a battle or a war, were cut to pieces, the suckling children torn from their mothers' breasts and delivered to the slaughter, and with milk still in their mouths their necks were driven through by the sword.[7]

What could be more horrendous than this tragedy? These things were done by the one seeking to destroy Jesus, and the long-suffering God bore this most insufferable tragedy, with its massive bloodshed, even though he could have prevented it, thus showing forth his great long-suffering for some inscrutably wise purpose.

d   When he returned from the barbarian land and grew up, war was rekindled against him on every side. First, the disciples of John [the Baptist] envied him, being jealous of him, even though John himself was devoted to him. So they said, "The one who was with us beyond the Jordan—behold, he is now baptizing, and all are coming to him."[8] These were the words of men provoked in spirit, stirred with envy, and consumed by that passion. For the same reason also, one of John's disciples, the one who had said these things, having a contentious spirit, argued with one of the Jews about the issue of

---

[7]Referring to the slaughter of the innocents by King Herod (Mt 2.16–18).
[8]Jn 3.26.

purification, comparing one kind of baptism with another—the baptism of John with that of the disciples of Christ: "A question arose," says the evangelist, "between the disciples of John and a certain Jew concerning purification."[9]

E   And when he began performing miracles, how many slanderers there were! Some called him a Samaritan, and demon-possessed, saying, "You are a Samaritan, and you have a demon."[10] Others called him an imposter, saying, "This one is not from God, for he deceives the multitude."[11] Still others called him a sorcerer, saying, "It is by the prince of the demons, Beelzebub, that he casts out demons."[12] They repeated these things continually, as well as calling him an enemy of God, a glutton, voracious, a drunkard, and a friend of the wicked and depraved: "The Son of Man has come," says the evangelist, "eating and drinking"; and so they say, "Behold the man, a glutton and a [553] winebibber, and a friend of tax collectors and sinners."[13] And when he spoke with a prostitute, they called him a false prophet: "For if he were a prophet," one said, "he would know who this woman is who is speaking with him."[14]

Each day they gnashed their teeth against him. And not only did the Jews fight against him in this way, but also those who were reputed to be his brothers did not treat him in a kind way; and by those of his own house war was rekindled against him. See how they also had been led astray, from the evangelist adding the remark, "Neither did his brothers believe in him."[15]

4.A   But since you call to mind how many now are stumbling and going off into error, how many of the disciples do you think stumbled

[9]Jn 3.25.
[10]Jn 8.48.
[11]Jn 7.12.
[12]Mt 9.34.
[13]Lk 7.21.
[14]Lk 7.39.
[15]Jn 7.5.

at the time [*kairos*] of the cross? For one betrayed him, others ran
away, and another denied him; and when all of them had fled, he was
led away, bound, and alone. How many of those who had previously
seen the signs he was doing—raising the dead, cleansing the lepers,
driving out demons, multiplying bread, and working other wonders—now at that time were scandalized at seeing him held captive
and bound, surrounded by common soldiers, with the Jewish priests
following and making a great disturbance and tumult, and all his
enemies carrying him off, having him alone in their midst, and with
the traitor standing by and exulting in his deed?

And then, what do you think was the effect on the crowd as he
was being whipped? It seems likely that there was then an innumerable multitude of them who were scandalized. Moreover, it was a
festival that had gathered everyone together, and it was the capital
city that welcomed the drama of lawlessness, and it happened in the
very middle of the day.

B   How many do you think were then scandalized upon seeing
him bound, scourged, streaming with blood, subjected to examination at the tribunal of the governor, and with not one of his disciples
standing by?—and when such varied scenes of derision against him
unfolded continually, one after the other: when they crowned him
with thorns, when they wrapped him in a robe, when they put a reed
in his hand, and when they fell to the ground, prostrating themselves
before him, mocking him and shaming him in so many ways?

How many do you think were scandalized, how many were
bewildered, how many were confounded when they slapped him
on the cheek, and said, "Prophesy to us, Christ; who is it who struck
you?"[16]—and when they led him back and forth, and made him
endure all day long these mockeries and insults and abuse and
derision and laughter, in the midst of the Jews who were watching
it all?—and when the servant of the high priest slapped him?—and
when the soldiers divided his garments?—and when they stretched

[16]Mt 26.68.

him on the cross, naked, and bearing on his back the marks of the scourging, and then crucified him? Not even at that moment were these savage beasts softened, but they became even more frenzied than before, and the tragedy intensified, and their mockery increased.

C   Then some of them said, "Behold the one who destroys the temple and in three days raises it up!"[17] And others said, "He saved others; he cannot save himself."[18] Still others said, "If you are the Son [554] of God, come down from the cross, and we will believe in you."[19]

And how many do you think were scandalized when they offered him gall and vinegar to drink on a sponge, insulting him? And when the thieves reviled him? And how many shuddered in horror at this extreme height of lawlessness, when this thief, this brigand, guilty of a myriad of crimes worthy of death, was deemed more worthy of pity than he; and hence Barabbas was chosen, contrary to the advice of the judge, as they wished to bestow honor on the evildoer rather than on Christ? They reckoned that by doing this they were proving that he was worse than the thief, and that they would not save him out of kindness, or out of consideration for the feast. They did all this to discredit any esteem that any of the onlookers may have had for him. And so, on account of this, they crucified him between two thieves.

D   But the truth was not obscured, but shone forth all the more brightly.

In addition, they accused him of tyranny, saying, "He who makes himself a king speaks against Caesar."[20] Against the one who had no place to lay his head, they brought an accusation of tyranny. And they denounced him for blasphemy. The high priest tore his garment

[17]Mt 27.40.
[18]Mt 27.42a.
[19]Mt 27.42b.
[20]Jn 19.12.

while saying of him, "He has blasphemed! What further need do we have for witnesses?"[21]

And his death, how was it? Was it not the death of condemned criminals? Was it not the death of those who are cursed? Was it not most shameful? Was it not the death of those who commit offenses that reach the very limit of lawlessness, who are not worthy to live, or even to draw their last breath on this earth?

E   And the manner in which he was placed in the tomb—was that not accomplished from charity? For someone came and begged for his body. And yet the one who buried him was not one who was close to him, nor one of those whom he had ministered to, nor one of his disciples, nor one of those who had enjoyed salutary association with him. For all those had become fugitives; all those had abandoned him.

And when that evil suspicion was concocted against the resurrection, with the claim that "his disciples came and stole him,"[22] how many were scandalized, how many were tripped up then? And this story prevailed for a time, even though it had been invented, and purchased with a sum of money. And it continued to prevail among some, even after the seals of the tomb had been broken, even after the truth of the resurrection was made manifest all around. For the multitude did not grasp the teaching about the resurrection, especially since at that time his disciples did not believe either. "For they did not understand then," says the evangelist, "that it was necessary for him to rise from the dead."[23] How many, therefore, do you think were scandalized in those days? But still, the long-suffering God endured it, ordering everything by his own ineffable wisdom.

5.A   And after those days the disciples were again in hiding, escaping [555] notice, fugitives, fearful, trembling, continually moving from one

[21]Mt 26.65.
[22]Mt 28.13.
[23]Jn 20.9.

place to another to remain unnoticed. After fifty days they appeared openly, and began working wonders, but even then they did not enjoy security. And even after those days, there were a myriad of stumbling-blocks [*skandala*] to trip up the weaker brethren—when they were flogged, and with the Church shaken, and they themselves harassed, and their enemies dominating everywhere and causing tumults.

When, through the miracles they worked, they gained much boldness of speech, then the death [*teleutē*] of Stephen unleashed a horrendous persecution, with everyone scattered, and the Church plunged into turmoil. And again the disciples lived in fear, again they were put to flight, again they suffered in agony.

B   Yet during this time the affairs of the Church prospered, as she flourished in the midst of miracles, shining forth brilliantly as she did from the beginning. For instance, one disciple was let down through a window and so escaped from the hands of the ruler.[24] Others an angel set free and delivered from their chains.[25] Others were given hospitality by merchants and artisans when they were hounded by those in power. They were well-treated by all—women sellers of purple, tentmakers, tanners, those living far from the cities, by rivers, and by the sea.[26] Often they did not dare to appear in the cities; and if they did risk this, those providing them hospitality did not.

C   So it was that the fabric of the Church was woven, whether in the midst of trials or in times of respite. And those who stumbled in the beginning were afterwards corrected, and those who had gone astray were brought back, and the ruined places were restored to higher heights. And so, when Paul asked that the preaching of the gospel only proceed smoothly, the all-wise and benevolent God did

[24]Acts 9.25 (cf. 2 Cor 11.33).
[25]Acts 12.5–17; 16.25–34.
[26]Lydia was a seller of purple (Acts 16.14–15), Priscilla and Aquila were tentmakers (Acts 18.3), and Simon was a tanner (Acts 9.43).

not yield to his disciple. And even though he prayed often, God did not grant his request, but said, "My grace is sufficient for you; for my power is perfected in weakness."[27]

D   Therefore, if you wish now to reckon up the pleasant things along with those that are sorrowful, you will see that many events have happened which, if not signs and wonders, still resemble signs, and are ineffable proofs of the great providence of God and his solicitude. But if everything you are hearing from us is not immediately providing you comfort, I leave things to your consideration, so that you may very carefully analyze everything and make a comparison of these things with your reasons for sadness, and through this good effort you may lead yourself away from despondency. For you will gain much consolation through this.

E   Please convey many kind words from us to all your blessed household. May you continue in good health and good spirits, my most venerable and most God-beloved lady.

        If you wish me to write further, make it clear to me, without deceiving me, that you have thrown off all despondency, and that you are living in serenity. For if these letters of mine are a medicine [556] for you, producing in you much joy, you will see me writing to you continually. But do not write to me again that you have much consolation from my letters, for this I already know. Instead, write to me that which I desire—that you are not disquieted, that you are not weeping, but rather that you are living in serenity and joy.

---

[27] 2 Cor 12.9.

From Cucusus, after six months in exile very shortly after the previous letter

Late 404

1.A The letter which I recently sent to Your Graciousness ought to [556] be sufficient to keep in check the inflammation of your distress. But since the tyranny of despondency has so thoroughly prevailed over you, I consider it necessary to add a second letter to the preceding one, so that you may have consolation in overflowing abundance, and that from now on your health may be firmly secured.

B Come now, therefore, and I will scatter the dust of your despondency by another means, for I know that this "dust" has resulted from a grievously swelling wound in your soul. And I must not be negligent in my care for you, since dust, if it is not brushed away quickly, can cause the greatest harm to the most precious of our organs, the eye—completely interfering with one's vision. Lest such a thing happen to you, let us make haste, and with great care tend to the malady afflicting you.

So rise up, and extend your hand to me. Typically, among those who suffer physically, if the doctors overlook something in their examination, the patient's health is compromised. So also this can happen when it is the soul that is agitated. [C] So that such a thing will not happen with you, hasten to bring to us your own self-examination, as is fitting for you with your high intelligence. This will be exceedingly helpful for both of us.

"I would like to," you may say, "but I'm not able, for I have not succeeded in shaking off the dense cloud and darkness of despair which greatly overshadow me."

But this is just an excuse and a pretext! For I know well the nobility of your thoughts, I know the strength of your soul that is filled with piety, I know the greatness of your intelligence, and the power of your Christian way of thinking [*philosophia*] which alone is sufficient to command the madness of your despair to be cast into the sea, making everything calm.

D But in order for this to happen more easily, we will make our own examination for ourselves. And what can you do to make this happen readily? Carefully consider all the things I wrote to you in my previous letter (for we said many things there on this subject); and along with that, do what I am now enjoining you to do. And what is that? When you hear that among the churches, one has sunk, another is shaken, another is beaten by fearsome waves, another has suffered irreparable damage, one has received a wolf instead of a shepherd, and another a pirate instead of a pilot, and another an [557] executioner instead of a doctor, then grieve (for it is not possible to bear such things without being pained)—yes, grieve, but *set a limit to your grief.*

E For if, concerning our own sins, for which we are about to be held accountable, it is not necessary or safe, but rather it is greatly ruinous and hurtful, to grieve with much excessiveness, much more is it exaggerated and vain to grieve excessively concerning the sins of others—which leave us enfeebled and bruised. This is something satanic, ruinous for the soul.

2.A And in order that you may know that these things are so, I am going to recount a story from former times. There was a certain man in the church of Corinth who was enjoying sacred things in great abundance, who had been purified through the mystery of baptism, and who had partaken in the most awesome eucharistic banquet, and who had shared entirely in all of our sacred mysteries (many say he held the position of a teacher). After this holy initiation, and after being a partaker of all these ineffable good things, and after having held the first place in the church, he fell into a most horrendous sin. Beholding the wife of his father with culpable eyes, he did not restrain his evil desire, but allowed his debauched thought to be accomplished. And it was not only adultery that he dared to commit, but many even more horrendous deeds of sexual immorality.

B The blessed Paul, having heard about this, but not having a word to use to describe the sin adequately, refers to the enormity of the lawlessness in another way, saying, "It is said that there is an evil in your midst, that is so impure that it cannot be named."[1] He did not say, "he did not dare to commit it," but, "one cannot even name it," thus wishing to show forth the enormity of the lawless act. And after delivering the sinner over to the devil, he cut him off entirely from the Church, commanding that he not by any means be allowed to partake in fellowship. For Paul said that it was not right to eat together with such a one, whom he subjected to this most extreme punishment, turning him over to the devil for his flesh to be cut up in pieces.

C However, Paul, having cut him off from the Church, and having forbidden him to have fellowship, ordered everyone in the church to be in mourning for him. "For you are puffed up," he told them, "and you have not been grieving; hence the one who did that deed must be taken up out of your midst."[2] The one who drove that man away from everyone as a plague, the one who entirely shut him out of the house, the one who delivered him to Satan, the one who subjected him to such punishment, when he saw the man afflicting himself in repentance, and making retribution to those whom he had sinned

[1] 1 Cor 5.1.
[2] 1 Cor 5.2.

against, then changed the way he was dealing with him, and commanded the opposite. For the one saying, "Cut off, turn back, be in mourning, and let the devil receive him"—what does he also say? "Express love toward him, lest he be overtaken with too much grief, lest he be conquered by Satan; for we are not ignorant of his wiles."[3] Do you see how afflicting yourself without measure is a satanic work [558] and a trap of the evil one, turning a salutary remedy into something destructive due to a lack of moderation?

D   And it did become something destructive to the man who was given over to the devil when he fell into immoderation. Therefore Paul said, "So that we might not be vanquished by the devil." In other words, he is saying this: "The sheep was covered with disease, so it was isolated from the others; it was separated from the Church in order for the disease to be treated, so that the sheep might be restored to its former condition; for such is the power of repentance. And so it is for the rest of our flock. Let us draw him to ourselves with one accord; let us welcome him with open arms; let us embrace him; let us envelop him; let us bring him into our midst. And if we do not wish to do this, the devil will gain the advantage over us, taking one who was not his but rather was one of ours, who because of our neglect of him was thrown into the sea out of an excess of grieving, making him the devil's from now on." Therefore he added, "For we are not ignorant of his wiles," since often, through becoming too involved with attending to routine matters, those who are not attentive are tripped up.

3.A   If on behalf of those committing sins—even such a sin as this— and on behalf of others committing sins for which they will have to give account, Paul does not allow the sinner to be engulfed in too much remorse, but rather hastens and rises up and does everything he can to cut off the weight of despondency, saying that immoderation is satanic, a triumph of the devil and of his evil-doing, a work

[3] 2 Cor 2.7, 11.

of evil thoughts, how is it not the height of insanity and madness to let yourself be torn to pieces and to suffer as one whose mind is enveloped in indescribable darkness, in much turbulence, confusion, tumult, and inexpressible distress? If you tell me again, "I want to prevail over these things, but I don't have the strength to do so," once again I tell you, "This is just an excuse, a pretext!"—for I know the vigor of your philosophic soul.

B   From another angle, in order that I might make it easier for you to take a stand against and vanquish this untimely and dreadful despondency, do once again what I prescribe for you to do. When you hear someone describing this universal ruination, flee quickly from thoughts [*logismōn*] about it, and hasten to meditate on the fearsomeness of the Last Day, and ponder within yourself the fearful judgment seat: the judge who cannot be bribed, the rivers of fire flowing before that tribunal, bubbling with an all-devouring flame, the sharpened swords, the harsh punishments, the endless chastisement, gloom without a glimmer of light, the outer darkness, the poisonous worm, the unbreakable chains, the gnashing of teeth, the inconsolable groaning, and the spectacle of the entire world—or rather, the spectacle of both created worlds, the one above and the one below: "And the powers of the heavens will be shaken," says the Scripture.[4] For if no one understands these things, nor the approaching rendering of accounts, nevertheless, one cannot see the entire race of men and innumerable people being judged without standing [559] there in fear. Yes, there will be great fear then. Therefore, meditate on these things, and on the inescapable judgments.

C   For that judge will have no need of accusers, neither of witnesses, neither of demonstrations, neither of proofs; but everything that has ever been done he will bring into the open, before the eyes of all those who have sinned. At that time, no one will have anyone standing by to rescue him from the torments—neither father, nor

[4]Mt 24.29.

son, nor daughter, nor mother, nor any other relative, nor any neighbor, nor any friend, nor any advocate, nor any gift of money, nor any abundance of wealth, nor any amount of power—for all these things will be scattered far away like dust, and the one being judged will abide alone, with only his deeds to absolve or condemn him. At that time, no one will be judged for another's sins, but only for his own.

D   Therefore, having gathered together all these considerations, and after having stirred up this fear, then, placing a stronghold against satanic and soul-damaging grief, stand fast in battle array against it, and so you will be able to scatter it more easily than a spider's web. This grief, besides the fact that it is vain and excessive, is exceedingly destructive and hurtful, while that fear which I'm speaking of is needful, useful, and advantageous, having great profit.

However, it has not escaped my notice that I have been swept away by the torrent of my words; I have given you counsel which has not been fitting for you. For me, and for those who have been swamped with sins against me, this word is necessary, for it works effectively through fear. But you, who are adorned with such great virtue and have already touched the vault of heaven, do not need to be spurred on in this way.

Therefore, I will compose another melody to use in conversing with you; I will arrange a prelude in another key—for this fear is not able to stir you, except in the measure that it can stir the angels. So now we are making a change! Come, and make a change in reasoning yourself, and consider the rewards due to you for your great accomplishments of virtue—the gleaming prizes, the brilliant crowns, the choir of virgins, the sacred palaces, the heavenly bridal chamber, life with the angels, intimate communion with the heavenly bridegroom, and that marvelous procession of torchbearers—those who excel in speech and thought.

4.A   Do not interrupt my discourse, even if I have included you in the chorus of sanctified virgins while you are living in widowhood.

For you have heard me speak often, both privately and in public, about the definition of virginity, such that no one would prevent you from being included in the choir of virgins, since you have surpassed many in that state by showing forth your great wisdom [*philosophia*] in other ways. On account of this, Paul set forth a definition of virginity by which he called a virgin not someone unmarried, or someone who never had relations with a man, but rather one who is devoted to the things of God.[5]

Christ himself has shown how much greater than virginity is [560] almsgiving [*eleēmosynē*]—in which you hold the scepter, for which you have repeatedly earned a crown. Half the virgins lost their part in that choir, since they entered without almsgiving—or rather, since they did not possess it in abundance. For they did have oil [*elaion*], but not enough.[6] Those who came without virginity, because they were replete with charity, were welcomed with much honor, being called "blessed of the Father";[7] and being called this by him, they were graced with their inheritance in the kingdom, and were proclaimed in the midst of the earth. He did not hesitate, in the presence of the angels and all of creation, to call them nourishers and givers of hospitality.

B   You also, you will hear this blessed word, you will enjoy the recompense for what you have given with great profusion. For if for almsgiving alone there are such rewards, such crowns—so brilliant, so illustrious, so glorious—and if I remind you of your other works of virtue, *what excuse will you have*, when henceforth you ought to be keeping festival—leaping, and dancing, and wearing a crown—if, like one who goes mad, or like one who casts himself off a cliff, cutting himself in pieces, you offer easy access into your holy soul

---

[5]Cf. 1 Cor 7.34; St Basil the Great expressed the same notion in reverse: "I have not known a woman, yet I am not a virgin" (quoted by St John Cassian, *Institutes* 6.19); St Gregory of Nyssa likewise explored a non-bodily notion of virginity in his *On Virginity*.

[6]Cf. Mt 25.1–12.

[7]Cf. Mt 25.34.

to the devil, who has never stopped tormenting you until this very day?

c   How can one adequately describe your patience—demonstrated in many ways, under many aspects and forms? And what discourse, for what length of time, would be sufficient for us to recount all your sufferings from your earliest youth until now—sufferings coming from those in your household, from strangers, from friends, from enemies, from those related to you by birth, from those who are not related to you, from the powerful, from commoners, from rulers, from those involved in secular affairs and from those invested in the ranks of the clergy? A recounting in detail of each one of these trials would be sufficient to comprise an entire history.

d   If someone would wish to turn to other aspects of this virtue of yours, and recount not just the sufferings brought on by others, but also those brought on by yourself, what stone, what iron, what steel would he not find which you have not conquered? For having received tender and delicate flesh, and having been raised with every sort of delicacy, you have been as unaffected in fighting against your manifold sufferings as one who is dead. Yet now you have aroused within yourself such a swarm of maladies that the art of doctors, and the power of medicines, and every kind of care have been confounded, as long as you continue to live in inner turmoil.

5.a Your firmness, your self-control in that which concerns eating and sleeping—if someone wished to describe these things, how would he find words to do so? Moreover, you have not permitted anyone, so to speak, to refer to your self-control and firmness using these terms, for your virtues are so much greater that we must search for other names for them. Because in referring to someone's self-control and firmness, we speak of one who, being tormented [561] by a passion, controls it. But you, you have nothing to control, for from the beginning you have possessed great ardor against the flesh, quenching its desires. You have not bridled the horse, but have tied its feet and thrown it to the ground, while remaining completely unmoved.

B   After having succeeded in self-control, now you are succeeding in *apatheia*.[8] For the desire for luxury does not trouble you, and you do not have to work to control it. But having once and for all suppressed this desire, and having rendered your flesh impervious to it, you have taught your stomach to be content with only as much food and drink as you need to not die, and to not suffer [bodily] affliction. This is why I do not call your fasting and your self-control by these terms, but by something else greater.

C   This can also be seen in your holy vigils. For you have quenched the desire for sleep along with quenching the desire for food. And you have destroyed it by another means, for from the beginning you subjected your nature to violence, spending entire nights without sleep. Later, through the force of long habit, you turned your practice into something natural. Just as it is natural for others to sleep, for you it is natural to keep vigil.

These things are marvelous, causing astonishment, even when just considered in themselves. But when one examines the circumstances surrounding these practices—that you practiced this asceticism from your earliest youth, that you did not have any teacher to instruct you, that you scandalized a great number of people, that from the spiritual point of view you are now living in an impious setting devoid of the truth, and that you have accomplished all this in a woman's body made even more delicate by the fame and luxury of your parents—how great an ocean of wonders will become manifest if someone reveals them one by one? For this reason I will not make mention of your humility, your love, and the rest of the virtues of your holy soul. For the moment I recall these things and

[8]*Apatheia* refers to the virtue of being detached from inordinate desire for earthly things.

make mention of them, my mind gushes forth like a fountain with a myriad of thoughts of other virtues of yours, and I feel constrained to speak about them in detail as I have above—or to mention only their most important aspects, for otherwise my discourse would continue on without limit.

D But it is not fitting for me to speak only about the chief aspects of your virtues—as I've just said, so that I might not be borne upon a limitless sea. This is because it is meant for me to pull your despondency out by the roots. So I will gladly draw out my words and sail upon an endless sea—and especially this sea, which opens up the multiple paths of each of your virtues, with each of these paths bringing forth more paths: whether it be your patience, or your humility and multi-faceted almsgiving stretching even to the ends of the earth, or your love surpassing in burning fervor a myriad of furnaces, or your boundless intelligence filled with much grace, all surpassing the measure of nature. If anyone would wish to enumerate all the ways your virtues have borne fruit, he would be like someone trying to count the waves of the sea.

6.A Therefore, while sailing on this endless sea, I am constrained "to show the lion by its claws,"[9] by commenting on just a few details of your apparel, of the clothing that you wear simply and without deliberation. These details might seem to be of little importance compared with other aspects of your piety, but if one examines them [562] carefully, one finds that they are great, manifesting a wisdom-loving soul, one that is trampling upon the things of this life, and pressing hard toward the things of heaven.

B This is why, not only in the New Testament, but also in the Old, when God leads the race of men through shadows and types, governing this world in more material ways, with no one making

[9]A proverb indicating that something can be made known by describing one part of it.

any mention of heavenly things, neither of things that are about to occur, and without employing the enigmatic language of true wisdom, but rather through the denser and more fleshly-oriented laws written for the Hebrews, in which exaggerated concern for clothing is vehemently forbidden, he states through the prophet, "This is what the Lord says about the daughters of Zion: 'Because their daughters have proudly lifted themselves up, because they walk with their necks outstretched, with a wanton look in their eyes, and with their robes rustling with the sway of their stride, making a jingling with their feet, the Lord will abase the daughters of the great ones of Zion. He will reveal what is beneath their outward appearance, he will take away the glory of their apparel.' 'Instead of sweet perfume there will be ashes; instead of a sash you will live with a rope; instead of adornment for your head you will have baldness on account of your works; and instead of a tunic adorned with purple you will have sackcloth.'"[10]

This is what you will have instead of your own embellishments. Do you see the ineffable anger? Do you see the most extreme punishment and anguish? Do you see the fierce captivity? From all of this you can determine the magnitude of the sin. For the one who loves mankind [*ho philanthrōpos*] never inflicts such severe punishment unless the sin that prompts it is not much greater still.

c   But if the sin is great, it is clear that the virtue that stands over against it is greater. This is why Paul, in addressing worldly-minded women, not only forbids adornment with gold, but also the wearing of sumptuous clothing.[11] For he knows, he knows full well, that this is a dreadful malady of the soul which is difficult to fight against, for it is paradigmatic of a corrupted will, while overcoming it is a sign of a most philosophic soul. This is all addressed not only to worldly-minded women, and to those who have relations with men—among whom there is scarcely anyone who accepts this

[10]Is 3.16–18, 24.
[11]Cf. 1 Tim 2.9.

exhortation easily—but also to those who seem to be living according to Christian wisdom [*philosophein*], and who seem destined to
be part of the choir of virgins.

D   For there are many who have stripped for the contest against
the tyranny of nature, who with purity are pursuing the path of
virginity, who in this mortal body are showing forth the precepts
of the resurrection: "for in the resurrection," he says, "they neither
marry nor are given in marriage."[12] And having engaged the battle
against the spiritual powers,[13] they contend eagerly for incorruption
in bodies that are corruptible, and—what is unbearable for many to
hear—they actually reach perfection through their works. For they
drive off their passion, which is like a ceaselessly leaping, frenzied
dog; and they take command over the raging ocean, sailing calmly
[563]   amidst the fierce waves, making a successful voyage across the
greatly troubled sea; and they stand firm in the furnace of physical
desire without being singed, trampling on the hot coals as if they
were clay. Yet, it can happen that such ones, capable of such great
things, can be viciously attacked, shamelessly and pitiably, by this
passion, and they can be conquered by it.

7.A   Virginity is something so great, and demands so much effort,
that Christ came down from heaven in order to make men like
angels and to implant the angelic way of life here below—not, however, daring to make this way of life mandatory, or to raise it to the
level of a law, but instead, instituting the law of self-mortification. Is
there anything that exists more burdensome than this? He has made
it a commandment to bear one's cross continually, and to do good to
one's enemies; but he has not made it a law to remain a virgin. He has
left this to the choice of those hearing Jesus' words: "The one who is
able to accept this, let him accept it."[14] For great is the weightiness of

[12]Mt 22.30.
[13]Cf. Eph 6.12.
[14]Mt 19.12.

this matter, and the difficulty of these struggles, and the sweat of the battles; and in pursuing this virtue the terrain is precipitous.

B   All this is shown forth by those under the Old Covenant who accomplished many acts of virtue. Moses, that great man, the chief of the prophets, a genuine friend of God, who enjoyed such boldness that he was responsible for rescuing six thousand men from the plague, the punishment commanded by God himself—this man was so powerful that he commanded the sea, parted the waves, shattered rocks, changed the air,[15] turned the water of the Nile into blood, sent forth against Pharaoh an army of frogs and locusts, transformed all of creation, and accomplished a myriad of other miracles and many deeds of virtue made manifest in various ways. Yet he did not have the strength to look in the face the combat involved with maintaining one's virginity. Rather, he had need of marriage, and the companionship of a wife and the security therein. Hence he did not dare to venture out upon the sea of virginity, fearing the waves thereof.

C   And the patriarch [Abraham], the one who was about to sacrifice his child, had the strength to vanquish the most tyrannical of natural feelings, being ready to kill his own child, his son Isaac who was in the flower of his age, at the height of youthfulness, his only-begotten genuine son, the one who was granted to him beyond all hope. Because of Isaac, Abraham was in great distress, being extremely advanced in age; and yet being intent on much virtue, he had the strength to lead his son up the mountain, being ready to commit such a deed. He built an altar, gathered wood, and placed the victim upon it. Then, seizing a knife, he placed the blade against the throat of the lad.

Yes, yes, that man of steel—nay, stronger than steel—placed his son on the altar and drew his blood. Steel possesses its strength by

---

[15]Perhaps referring to the swarms of flies filling the air in Egypt (Ex 8.21); or the fire, rain, and hail coming down from the heavens (Ex 9.23); or the darkness covering the land for three days (Ex 10.22). Or perhaps St John has all of these incidents in mind here.

nature; while with this man, it was through his wisdom and his will that he imitated the natural strength of that strongest of substances, and demonstrated through his works the *apatheia* of angels. And yet, even though he had the strength to finish such a great and important contest, surpassing the bonds of nature, still he did not dare to strip [564] down for the contest of virginity, fearing to enter the lists thereof, and instead accepted the consolation of marriage.

8.A As another example, do you wish that I bring forward Job?—the just, the true, the God-fearing, the one who fought hard against all the machinations of the evil one. This Job blinded the devil [by dazzling him with the light of virtue]; and being struck rather than striking, he emptied the devil's quiver as he was pierced ceaselessly by his arrows, enduring every kind of temptation, with each one more extreme than the one before it. For among the things that seem to be painful are, most especially, poverty, and sickness, and the loss of children, and the hostility of enemies, and the misunderstanding of friends, and hunger, and continual bodily pains, and outrages, and slanders, and gaining a bad reputation. All these evils were poured out upon one body and prepared for one soul; and yet the most grievous part was that all these things befell one who was not prepared for them.

B   This is what I mean to say: one who is born to poor parents and raised in a poor home, having been trained and prepared, can easily bear the burden of poverty. But someone who is surrounded with good things and decked with riches, upon suddenly falling into an opposite condition, cannot calmly bear the change. For one who is untrained, it appears to him to be all the more painful when he is attacked.

And again, one who is undistinguished, born of undistinguished parents, and who is used to living in wretched circumstances, will not be greatly troubled when he is injured and abused. Whereas one who enjoys glory, who is waited upon and talked about by everyone, who is seen everywhere and proclaimed by many, if he is brought down into dishonor and vileness, he suffers as someone rich suddenly becoming poor.

And for someone losing a child, even if he loses all of them, since they are not all lost at the same time, he has the consolation of the ones remaining for the ones lost. And having borne the suffering of losing the first one, if a second one is lost afterwards, for him the sorrow will be easier to bear, since it won't be a blow upon a new wound, but one that has already been healed and has disappeared. So the new pain will not last as long.

C But here is a man who saw his entire chorus of children snatched away in one moment, whose end came in the most bitter way. For their death was violent and premature, and the time and the place of the tragedy added not a little to his suffering. For it was at the hour of a meal, in a house open to entertaining strangers, when this house became a tomb for them.

And what can be said about his strange hunger? Who can explain it? Was it voluntary or involuntary? I do not know what to call it; neither can I find a name to give to this strange and unexpected situation. [D] He turned away from the table that was prepared for him; he did not touch the food he beheld. For the wounds that covered his body issued forth such a foul odor, giving the food a repugnant character, that his appetite was taken away. In describing all this he said, "For I behold my food as rottenness."[16] On the one hand, the constraint of his hunger was driving him to touch what was set before him; but on the other hand, the excessively foul odor issuing from his flesh overcame the power of his hunger.

This is why I said, "I do not know what to call it." Was it voluntary? But he did desire to taste what was before him. Was it involuntary? But the food was there, and no one was preventing him from having it. [565]

---

[16]Job 6.7.

How can one explain his suffering?—the multitude of worms, the oozing pus, the reproaches of friends, being despised by his servants—for he said: "My servants have not spared me; they have spit in my face."[17] Who trampled him under their feet? Who hurled themselves at him? "Those whom I esteem not to be worthy to be among the dogs with my flocks," he said, "those least of all men, who are now falling upon me and chastising me."[18] Don't all these things seem to you to be grievous? Indeed, they are grievous.

E   Should I tell you the chief of the evils, the pinnacle of the events that were strangling him the most? It was the storm of agitations that occurred in his mind—this is what especially choked him unbearably, producing an inner storm within his pure conscience, darkening his mind and troubling his governing spirit. For those who are conscious of having committed many sins, if they suffer fearfully, in searching for a reason for their suffering, they realize that their own sins are the cause of the storm unleashed by their own heedlessness. Whereas for those who are not conscious of having done anything wrong, and are only aware of having done right, if they suffer such things, they reflect upon the doctrine of the resurrection, and consider the recompense for these things, knowing that these contests that are occurring are the basis for a myriad of crowns. But this righteous Job, not having any idea about the resurrection, was tormented all the more because he did not know the reason for his suffering. And so, because of this bewilderment, he was stung by the pains and the worms all the more.

F   And so that you might learn that this was so, when the God who loves mankind declared him worthy in giving the reason for these struggles—"it was in order to manifest you as righteous that these things flooded upon you"—then he breathed easier, as if he had never suffered from those pains, as is clear from what he then

[17]Job 30.10.
[18]Job 30.1.

uttered. For after he learned the reason, he still suffered, but he bore it nobly; and after having lost everything, he spoke those marvelous words: "The Lord gave, the Lord took away; as it pleased the Lord, thus it came to pass; blessed be the name of the Lord for all ages."[19]

9.A But it seems that my love for this man has borne me along further away from the subject that I proposed to take up earlier. After adding a few more words, I will touch again upon what I spoke of earlier. For even this tremendously great man, who trampled upon his natural needs, even he did not dare to engage in the combat which we were talking about, for he enjoyed a wife and became the father of numerous children. Such are the difficulties involved with a life of virginity—so elevated and so great are the battles, and the sweat thereof; and many are the nerve-stretching efforts that are demanded.

B   Indeed, many women who have stripped to enter this combat have not been victorious over the passion of adorning themselves with an abundance of garments; rather, they have been vanquished [566] more than women who live in the world. I'm not even speaking about the gold they wear, or their wearing of gold-encrusted silken garments, or their necklaces of precious stones.

This passion is something much more grievous than everything else. The disease of such women, the tyranny of this passion, is shown forth superabundantly by those who have strived against, fought against, and violently struggled to overcome through their simple, plain clothing the luxuriousness of those who deck themselves with gold and silken garments, who endeavor to appear to be more lovely than those who think that such luxuriousness is of no account. So the nature of this passion is shown to be pernicious, and noxious, concealing the depths of perdition.

[19]Job 1.21.

c   I would need a myriad of mouths to adequately proclaim to you this fact, that what is so difficult for virgins to accomplish, this you are accomplishing in your widowhood so easily, without difficulty—the truth of which is proven by your deeds. I marvel not only at the indescribable simplicity of your attire, which surpasses that of the mendicants, but also the absence of form and artfulness in your clothing, your sandals, your gait. These are all the colors of your virtue, which depict outwardly the wisdom [*philosophia*] that abides in your soul. For "The clothing of a man," says the Scripture, "and the way he laughs and walks, announce the kind of person he is."[20] If you had not violently thrown down to the ground every earthly thought of the display of this world, trampling upon them, and if you had not reached such a degree of scorn for such thoughts, you would not have conquered that most grievous sin; you would not have cast it aside.

D   Let no one accuse me of exaggeration in calling this a most grievous sin. If it agitated the Hebrew women living in the world and brought with it such punishment at that time, if it now agitates our Christian women whose citizenship is in heaven,[21] who ought to be imitating the life of the angels, and who live in a state of grace, what excuse will they have who now dare to deck themselves out even more?

When you see a virgin walking languidly in her garments, letting her tunics ripple behind her—which the prophet condemned[22]— swaying in her gait; and with her voice, her eyes, and her attire mingling a deadly drink for those who look at her intemperately, and digging a deep pit for those approaching her, and thereby setting a trap; how could you call her a virgin, and not reckon her to be among the women of harlotry? For such virgins do not become

[20]Sir 19.27.
[21]Cf. Phil 3.20.
[22]Cf. Is 3.16.

an allurement any less than those women who openly unfurl their wings of pleasure.

E   On account of these things we esteem you to be blessed; on account of these things we marvel at you, that you have put all such things far away from yourself, showing yourself to be an example of mortification, not making a display of youthful beauty but of youthful courage, and not making yourself look beautiful, but taking weapons for battle.

10.A Up until now we have shown the lion by its claws, and this [567] only in part; for I have not yet rehearsed the whole ensemble of your virtues. For just as I said earlier, I fear to embark upon the boundless sea of all your other sterling attributes. We are not going to set forth an encomium for you in speaking of your holy soul; rather, we are going to prepare a remedy to encourage you. So come, as we take up again what we were speaking about earlier.

And what were we speaking about earlier? Putting aside consideration of how someone has sinned and how another has transgressed, think about your continual struggles, borne through your endurance, your patience, your fasting, your prayers, your sacred all-night vigils, your self-control, your almsgiving, your hospitality, your manifold trials, grievous and frequent. Consider how from your earliest youth to the present day you have not stopped nourishing Christ when he hungered, giving him drink when he thirsted, clothing him when he was naked, bringing him in when he was a stranger, taking care of him when he was sick, going to him when he was a prisoner.[23] Ponder upon the ocean of your love, which you have opened up to the very ends of the earth, spreading it with great alacrity. For it is not only your own house which you have opened to everyone coming to it; but everywhere, on earth and sea, many have enjoyed this honor, bestowed through your hospitality. Gathering all

[23]Cf. Mt 25.34–37.

these reflections, revel and rejoice in the hope of the crowns and the [heavenly] rewards for these things.

B   As for those who transgress the law, who shed blood, and who do many worse things, if you wish to see them punished, you will see this then. For Lazarus saw the rich man burning in hades. Even though according to the kind of life each one lived they were each in a different place, with an abyss separating them, with Lazarus in the bosom of Abraham while the other was in the unbearable furnace, nevertheless Lazarus saw him and heard his voice and responded to him.[24] Such things will be yours then.

C   If someone who only despised one man endured such torment, if for this one who only scandalized one person it would have been better if he had had a millstone placed around his neck and had drowned in the sea,[25] what of those who have scandalized the entire world, who have overturned churches, who have filled everything with tumult and affliction, who have surpassed robbers and barbarians in savagery and inhumanity, having yielded all their strength, in frenzied fury, to the authority of the devil and his accomplices the demons (according to the fearful teaching [of the Scriptures, which are] filled with sanctity, worthy of the one to whom it is given [to understand properly], but made a subject of derision by both Jews and Greeks)? What of these who have sunk a myriad of souls, who have caused a myriad of shipwrecks throughout the whole world, who have kindled fire, who have divided the body of Christ and have dispersed its members all around? "For you are," the Apostle says, "the body of Christ, and members one of another."[26]

But why am I contending ardently to show forth their madness, which is impossible to express in words? What kind of torments, do

[24] Cf. Lk 16.19–31.
[25] Cf. Mt 18.6.
[26] 1 Cor 12.27.

you think, then, are reserved for these destroyers, these drinkers of blood?

D   If those who did not give nourishment to Christ when he was hungry are condemned with the devil to the fire that never dies, [568] what about those who have reduced to famine choirs of monks and virgins, and have reduced to nakedness those who were clothed? And those who have not only not welcomed strangers but have chased them away; and those who have not only not cared for the sick but have afflicted them yet more; and those who have not only not visited the captives but have cast into prison those who had been free of chains? Imagine what torments they will suffer! Then, you will see them grilled, burning, enchained, weeping, their teeth gnashing, henceforth wailing futilely, and repenting uselessly and without recompense, just as that rich man. These same people will see you in the blessed state, crowned, chanting with the angels, reigning together with Christ; and they will cry out much, and wail, and repent of the inconsiderate words they said against you, addressing to you their supplications, and invoking your mercy and philanthropy. But all of this will be of no avail for them.

11.A Therefore, meditating on all these things, continually sing to your soul, and you will be able to scatter this dust. But since there is something else that particularly afflicts you, as I am aware, come and let us prepare a remedy for this thought [*logismō*], which we have spoken about earlier, and about which we will now speak further. For we know that you suffer not on account of these things only, but because you have been separated from our nothingness,[27] which causes you to weep continually and to say to everyone, "We no longer hear that voice of his, we no longer enjoy his teaching that we were so accustomed to. We are tortured by hunger. For that which God threatened to bring upon the Hebrews long ago, now we

---

[27]Chrysostom is speaking humbly of himself.

are enduring—'not a famine of bread, neither of water, but a famine of divine instruction.'"[28]

B What, therefore, shall we say about these things? That certainly it is possible for you, in my absence, to have fellowship with me through my books. And we will make haste, if we can locate couriers, to send you numerous, long letters. But if you desire to hear my living voice, perhaps this is possible, and we will see each other again, God willing—or rather, not "perhaps," but surely, without a doubt! For now, I will remind you that I have not said these things rashly—neither have I beguiled you, nor made a miscalculation—but that you may hear my living voice through my letters.

C If this plan saddens you, consider that it will not be without profit for you; nay, it will procure for you a great recompense, if you utter no bitter word about it, and if you glorify God because of this, even as you are continuing to do ceaselessly. This is no small contest; it requires an exceedingly vigorous soul and a philosophic mind, in order to bear the separation from a soul whom you love. Who is saying these things? If someone knows how to love genuinely, if he understands the power of love, he knows what I am saying.

[569] **D** But in order that we might not be slow in finding those who do love truly (for they are rare), let us run to the blessed Paul, who will tell us how great this struggle is, and how great the soul must be [to bear it]. For this Paul, who stripped down to his flesh, renouncing his body, and almost naked, encircled the whole world with his soul, having exiled from his mind every passion. And imitating the *apatheia* of the bodiless powers, and living on earth as if in heaven, and standing with the cherubim above, and taking part in their mystical song, he easily bore everything—enduring, as if he were in another's body, imprisonment, chains, arrests, scourgings, threats of death, stonings, dunkings, and every other kind of punishment.

[28]Cf. Am 8.11.

But when he was separated from one soul whom he especially loved, he was confounded and shaken to the point of immediately leaving the city in which he was waiting to see his beloved friend but not finding him there. That was Troas, which he left since his friend did not appear there. For as he said, "Having come to Troas for the sake of the gospel of Christ, a door having been opened unto me by Christ, I did not have rest in my spirit, since I did not find Titus my brother there. So I took leave of the brethren and departed for Macedonia."[29]

E   What is this, O Paul? Bound by a collar of wood, living in a prison, having scourgings laid upon you, with blood pouring forth on your back—you who have celebrated the mysteries, baptizing and offering the holy Eucharist, and never overlooking anyone wishing to be saved! Yet here you have come to Troas, and have seen the land cleared and ready to receive the seed, with yourself being very prepared to fulfill easily the role of a fisher of souls, and you have cast away the gain for which you came! "Having come to Troas for the gospel"—this means *on account of* the gospel; *and* with no one hindering, for he also says, "a door being opened to me." Yet you immediately turned away [from this opportunity], saying, "Nay, for I have been greatly seized by the tyranny of despondency; the absence of Titus has exceedingly distressed my mind, and it has so overpowered and dominated me that I am constrained to do this." What he suffered on account of despondency we have no need to conjecture about, for we have learned of it from him. For he lays out the reason for his departure in saying, "I did not have rest in my spirit, because I did not find Titus; so bidding them farewell, I departed."

12.A Do you see how great is the struggle to bear meekly a separation from someone you love? And how grievous and bitter this is? And how exalted and vigorous a soul it demands? This is the contest that you are now finishing. However great the contest is, the greater the

[29] 2 Cor. 2.12–13.

rewards, the more brilliant the crown. May what is coming to you be a consolation for you, and the fact that we will see you again, covered with flowers as your reward for this, and crowned, and proclaimed [570] to all. For neither does it suffice to be bound together with those we love only in soul, and neither does this suffice for our consolation, but rather to be also with them bodily; and if this be not added, by not a little is our happiness diminished.

B   But in coming again to the nurturing of love, we will find that this is so. For in writing to the Macedonians, he said, "We, brothers, having become orphaned [*aporphanisthentes*] from you for a time in presence, not in heart, endeavored more eagerly to see your face with great desire. Therefore we wanted to come to you—even I, Paul—time and again, but Satan hindered us. Therefore, when we could no longer endure it, we thought it good to be left in Athens alone, sending Timothy [to you]."[30] O the power of each word! For it shows forth with great clarity the flame of love stored up in his soul. For he did not say "separated," or "torn asunder," or "set at a distance," or "abandoned," but "*orphaned* from you." He found the exact word to emphasize the pain of his soul. And as he held the position of father for all of them, he uses the language of small orphans who have prematurely lost the ones who gave them birth, wishing to show forth the extremity of his despondency.

C   Nothing is more grievous than for children to be orphaned at a young age, being able to do nothing for themselves and having no one to be their lawful protectors. And when a large crowd appears, attacking them and laying traps for them, they are like sheep lying in the midst of wolves tearing them all apart and mangling them. No one is able to describe in words the magnitude of such misfortunes. Thus Paul, casting about in search of a word to convey the desolation and severity of such events, in order to describe what someone suffers when he is separated from his beloved friend, finds this word

[30] 1 Thess 2.17–18; 3.1–2.

to be sufficient, which he reinforces through what follows, when he says, "Having become *orphaned*, not for a long time, but just recently, and not in thought, but only concerning your physical presence, even so we could not endure the pain that resulted; and while having sufficient consolation in being bound together with you in spirit, and having you in our heart, and having seen you recently, still, nothing could free us from this despondency."

D But what do you want, O Paul, what do you desire, tell me—what do you desire with such great ardor? The actual sight of them. For he says, "For we hastened exceedingly to see your face."[31] What are you saying, O exalted and great one? You who consider the world to be crucified, and yourself crucified to the world?[32] You who are passing beyond everything that is fleshly, you who have become almost bodiless? Yet by your love, have you become a captive, to the point of being brought down to this flesh of clay, which is from the earth, perceived by the senses?

"Yes," he says, "and I am not ashamed to say these things—rather, I take pride in them; for having within me fruit-bearing love, which is the mother of all that is good, I seek these things. And not by chance do I seek their physical presence; indeed, it is *their face* that I *especially* desire to behold: 'For we hastened exceedingly to see [571] your face.'"

Therefore, do you long to see them, tell me, and do you desire to behold their face? "Very much so!" he says, "for that is where the organs of sense perception are gathered. For a disembodied soul, even while bound to another such soul, is not able to speak or hear. But when I am enjoying someone's physical presence, I can say something and can hear from those whom I love. This is why I desire to see your face; for it is there that the tongue sends forth the voice that expresses what is inside us, and the ears receive the words, and the eyes perceive in many colors the movements of the soul. Because

[31] 1 Thess 2.17.
[32] Cf. Gal 6.14.

of all this, I can enjoy more precisely the company of the soul that I ardently love."

13.A And in order for you to learn how he burned to see them, after saying "we hastened exceedingly," since this phrase was not strong enough, he added, "with much desire." Furthermore, he could not endure being mixed in with the others, so he indicated that he loves more intensely than the others by saying, "We hastened exceedingly, wishing to come to you." Thus, separating himself from the others, and standing alone, he added, "I, Paul, time and again," showing that he hastened more than the others.

Then, since he did not meet up with Titus, he sent to him, not letters, but what was most important to him, his companion Timothy, who would suffice for him instead of letters. Therefore, continuing on, he says, "Therefore no longer enduring. . . ." O once again the nobility of the phrase! O the power of these words, which indicate his ungovernable and unendurable love! And just as one who has been set on fire and is burning seeks protection from the flames. moving everything to find it, so this man, inflamed, suffocating, burning [with love], accordingly devised a way to find consolation for himself: "For no longer enduring," he says, "we have sent Timothy, the servant of the gospel and our fellow-worker. We were thus deprived of the company of our most valuable member, exchanging one pain for another." He could not easily bear the absence of that one; but for their sake he endures this heaviest sacrifice, which he indicates by saying, "I preferred to remain alone." O soul, which, to speak with exactness, was love itself!—since with the departure of a single brother, he says he was alone, even though he had these others with him.

B   Meditate always on these things, and consider that however much something is painful to you, by so much will it be more fruitful, if you bear it with thankfulness. This is true not only for wounds of the body, but also for wounds of the soul, which procure crowns which cannot be described when those who are so afflicted bear it with thanksgiving; for the distress of the soul is greater than that of the body. Just as, if your body is terribly lacerated and whipped, you bear it nobly, giving glory to God for this, you gain in return a great reward, so also if your soul suffers such things, you can await a vast recompense. Think about this: that if you saw us again, you would [572] be completely delivered from this pain; yet from this pain you will gain great profit, both in the future and in the present.

These thoughts ought to be sufficient for your consolation; and not for you only, but even for someone who is thoughtless and whose soul is hard as rock. But where there is great intelligence, and a treasure of piety, and a summit of wisdom [*philosophias*], and a soul that tramples on the fantasies of earthly things, the healing occurs much more easily.

c   You can demonstrate your love for us if you attribute to what we have written as much power as if we had been present with you. You will show this clearly, if we learn that you have become better through our letters—and not only better, but better by as much as we have greatly desired. And we have desired that your cheerfulness be as great now as that which we beheld in you when we were together. If we learn this, we will be abounding in fruitful consolation, even as we now abide in this solitude.

Therefore, if you wish to fill us with great joyfulness—which I know you wish for, and have zealously pursued—show us that you have completely chased away the burden of despondency, and that you are filled with calm. Give us this recompense for our love [*agapēs*] and care for you. For you know, you know well, how to rejuvenate [*anaktēsē*]³³ us—by succeeding in this, and demonstrating this with truthfulness in your letters to us.

---

³³Literally, "rebuild."

From Cucusus, after about seven months in exile

End of 404

1.A Why do you lament? Why do you smite yourself, afflicting [612] yourself with pains which even your enemies do not have the power to inflict upon you, as you give your soul over to the tyranny of despair? For the letters which you have sent to us through Patrikios have revealed the wounds of your heart and mind. Therefore I also am suffering great pain and distress, since when you must make every exertion and make it your business to shake off the despondency of your soul, you surround yourself with grievous thoughts [*logismous*], even inventing things which do not exist (as you have said), lacerating yourself in vain, for no purpose whatsoever, with great harm to yourself.

And why are you lamenting that you are not being able to get me relocated from Cucusus? You have moved mountains in trying to get this done. But as this has not come to pass, do not be in anguish about it. Perhaps it brings glory to God for me to be placed on a longer, double course,[1] so that the crowns may be brighter.

Why, therefore, should you suffer on account of the things that are declared about us, when you ought to leap, and sing in chorus, and be crowned, since we have been deemed worthy of these things that far surpass our merit? Is it the desolation of where I am now

---

[1] The Greek phrase refers to a race in which contestants run to the far end and back on a racecourse.

that grieves you? But what could be more pleasurable than to abide in this place, with tranquillity, calm, much leisure, and good physical health? And if this town has neither a marketplace [*agora*] nor a market, that is nothing to me. For everything flows to me as if from fountains. And I have my lord the local bishop, as well as my lord Dioscorus, who are devoting themselves entirely to my sustenance. The good Patrikios will tell you how we are abiding in joy, in good spirits, through the great solicitude that we have received ever since we began our sojourn here.

B   And if you are making lamentation about what happened to us in Caesarea, that also is unworthy of you. For there also, brilliant crowns were woven for us, such that everyone lauded us, praised us publicly, marveling and being astounded at all the evils we suffered from being sent into exile. But let no one know about these things [in Constantinople], even if there has been much talk spread abroad [613] about me. My lord Paeanius has disclosed to me that the priests of Bishop Pharetrius himself abide there, and that they are in communion with us, and are having nothing to do with those opposing us, neither associating with them nor being in communion with them. In order that we might not be a cause of distress to them, let no one know about these things.

Indeed, the things that have happened to us are exceedingly grievous. And even if we have no other dreadful thing to endure, the things that happened there suffice to procure for us a myriad of rewards, so extreme was the danger that we faced. I beseech you, then, let these things be unspoken by you, and I will describe things briefly to you myself, not in order for you to grieve, but that you may rejoice. For these things are my source of gain; this is my wealth, this is the recompense for my sins—that I journey on in the midst of such trials continually, and that these things are being inflicted upon me by those from whom they are in no way expected.

C   As we were about to enter the region of Cappadocia, after having escaped from that Galatian[2] who had threatened us nearly to the point of death, many people came to us on the way, saying, "The lord Pharetrius is waiting for you; and fearing lest he not meet up with you, he is doing everything he can to make sure he sees you, to embrace you, and to show all manner of love to you; and he has set the men's and women's monasteries in motion [to prepare for your arrival]." Upon hearing these things I expected nothing, and suspected within myself the opposite; so I said nothing to any of those who announced these things.

2.A   When finally, after a long time, we entered Caesarea, exhausted, withering away, lying there in the highest flame of fever, distraught, suffering in the furthest extreme, I came upon an inn, situated at the edge of the city, and I made haste to summon doctors who could tend to that furnace [of fever], which was now at its height. In addition to this, there was the exertion of traveling, the weariness, the strain, the dearth of any who could care for us, the lack of necessities, the absence of any physician for us, and the ravaging from fatigue, the heat, and sleeplessness. So being nearly dead, I thus entered the city.

Then arrived all the clergy, the people, monks and nuns, doctors; I received much solicitude; everything was done by everyone to minister to us and serve us. Despite all this, we were seized with a great increase in the flame [of fever]; we were in extreme danger. But in the end, the malady abated little by little. But Pharetrius was nowhere to be seen. He waited for our departure, but I do not know what his thoughts were.

B   When I saw that the malady was slowly diminishing, I desired to leave [Caesarea], in order to reach Cucusus, where I might enjoy some respite from the hardships of the journey. Yet while still there, news came that Isaurians in countless numbers were marauding in [614]

[2]Bishop Leontius of Ancyra.

the region of Caesarea; they had set a large village on fire, destroying it utterly. Upon hearing this, the tribune departed, taking his soldiers with him, for they feared an attack on the city. Everyone was in terror, everyone was in agony, for the very soil of their country was endangered; so even the old men of the town gathered to participate in the defense of its walls.

c   In the midst of all of this, suddenly, at dawn, a *horde* of monks— it's necessary to speak in this way, to indicate by this word their frenzy—stormed up to the house where we were, threatening to set it on fire, to burn it down, to reduce us to the last extremity if we did not come out. And neither fear of the Isaurians, nor the sickness that was ravaging me so fiercely, nor anything else could mollify them. Rather, their rage increased, so that even the soldiers guarding us were filled with fear. The monks continued to threaten the soldiers with blows, and exulted in already having shamelessly struck many of them.

d   Hearing these things, the soldiers sought refuge with us, beseeching and crying, "Even if we are about to fall into the hands of the Isaurians, deliver us from these beasts!" Hearing this, the governor ran to the house, wishing to help us. But the monks scorned his exhortations, so that even he weakened in resolve. Seeing the great difficulty of the situation, and, on account of the monks' fury, not daring to counsel us either to go out to a near-certain death or to stay inside, he sent for Pharetrius, begging him for several days' respite, on account of my sickness and the danger menacing us. But this accomplished nothing, for the monks then became more enraged, and not one of the priests dared to come to us and help us. Rather, flushed red with shame (for they said that all of this was occurring according to Pharetrius' intention), they lay hidden, unnoticed, and did not respond when we called for them.

E   Is it necessary to say more? Beset by these fears, with death nearly certain, and with the fever torturing me (for we were not yet delivered from all the evils there), at midday I threw myself onto a litter and got out of there, with all the crowd crying out, wailing, cursing the one responsible for these things, and with everyone groaning and lamenting.

F   Once I left the city, some of the clergy came out unobtrusively to accompany us along the way, mourning. We heard some of them saying, "Where are they leading him to a certain death?" Another one—one of those who love us very much—said, "Get away, I beg [615] you! Fall into the hands of the Isaurians, if you can get away from us! But wherever you fall, may you fall into safety, if you escape out of our hands." Having heard and seen these things, the good Seleukia, the wife of my lord Rufinus³ (who gave me great care), begged and besought me to stay at her villa in a suburb about five miles outside the city. She sent men to us, and we departed to go there.

3.A   But not even then was this plot against us to come to an end. For as soon as Pharetrius found out about it, he exposed it, as she said, with many threats against her. But when she received me in her villa, I knew nothing about that. Coming out to meet us, she concealed these things from us, but disclosed them to her steward, whom she ordered to furnish me with every means of rest. And if certain monks came to us, with the intention of insulting and mistreating us, he was to gather together laborers from her other estates to be set in battle array against them. She besought me to take refuge in her own home [located elsewhere], which had an impregnable fortress, that I might escape from the hands of the bishop and the monks.

B   But I did not accept her offer. Rather, I stayed in the villa, knowing nothing about what was being devised to come next. But this was

³The prefect of Constantinople. St John wrote one of his letters from exile to him with great affection.

insufficient to calm their fury against us. Then, at midnight, with me not knowing anything about this (for Pharetrius was continuing to assert much pressure, brandishing his threat, as she told me, constraining her, insisting that we be cast out from those suburbs), the woman, refusing to bear his oppressiveness, announced to me that the barbarians were invading. For she was embarrassed to have to tell me about Pharetrius' compulsion.

Then, in the middle of the night, the priest Evethius[4] came to me, shook me from my sleep, and with a very loud cry, said: "Arise! I beg you! The barbarians have invaded, and they are near here!" Imagine how this news struck me! Then I asked him what we needed to do, saying, "We cannot flee back into the city, lest we suffer something worse than what the Isaurians are about to do." So he compelled me to go out from there.

C   It was a moonless night. The entire night was gloomy and dark, which also made the situation critical for us. There was no one to assist us, no one to help, for everyone had abandoned us. Meanwhile, prodded by fear, expecting to be killed immediately, I resigned myself to the calamity, and called for torches to be lit. But that priest ordered that they be extinguished, lest perhaps the barbarians, drawn to us by the light, might attack us. So the torches were extinguished.

D   Then, the mule that was carrying me in the litter fell down on his knees (for the way was rough, steep, and rocky), dragging me, inside the litter, almost to the point of perishing. I jumped out of the [616] litter, supported by the priest Evethius (for he had also jumped down from his animal), and as he led me by the hand, I walked—or rather, I was dragged. For one could scarcely walk on such difficult terrain, amongst steep mountains, in the middle of the night.

E   Imagine how much I naturally suffered, encompassed by such evils—for the fever continued to harass me, and knowing nothing

[4]One of the local priests in Caesarea.

of what was being devised for me, and with trembling fearing the barbarians, expecting to fall into their hands. Does it not seem to you that these sufferings alone, even if I didn't experience any others, would have the power to loose me from many of my sins and provide a grand beginning of [divine] favor?

F   The cause, as I came to realize, of everything that happened since my arrival in Caesarea was that some of the magistrates, some of their assistants, some of the leading citizens, some of the tribunes, and all the people seeing me every day, all waited on me, considering me as the apple of their eye. I think it was this that provoked Pharetrius—so the jealousy that drove us from Constantinople has not refrained from pursuing us even here, it seems to me. I can't prove it, but I suspect this is the case.

And what can be said about the other trials along the way, the fears, the dangers? Yet remembering all of them every day, and having them always in my mind, I flutter with pleasure, I leap for joy as having a great treasure in reserve. In this, I am settled. And this is why I beseech you, most honored one, to rejoice in all these things, to be glad, to leap for joy, to glorify God who has deemed us worthy to suffer these things. And I beg you to keep these things to yourself, divulging them to no one, especially the soldiers who have the power to fill the entire city [with the story], though they themselves have been exposed to the most extreme dangers. So, let no one learn of these things from Your Piety, and impose silence on those who are saying anything.

4.A If you are grieving because of the aftermath of the evils I've experienced, know for certain that I have shaken them off completely, and that I am now in stronger physical health than before. And why are you anxious about the cold here? For we have been provided with a house adapted for that. And my lord Dioscorus is doing everything for me, making it his business to make sure that we do not suffer even a little bit from the cold. And if I may conjecture from this beginning, it seems to me that the climate now is oriental in nature, no less than that of Antioch—so great is the warmth, so great is the temperateness of the air.

B   But you have caused me great pain in saying, "Perhaps you are upset with us for neglecting you." Yet many days ago we wrote to you, [617] most honored one, beseeching you not to [try to] have me moved from here. I reckon now that you need to make a strong defense, with much sweat and trouble, in order to justify these words of yours. Perhaps you have justified your words in part by saying, "I am thinking this simply in order to increase my torment." But in my turn, I consider it a huge accusation [against you] that you should say, "I steadily increase my pain through these thoughts." For when you ought to be doing everything you possibly can to throw off your torment, you do the devil's will by increasing your despondency and grief. Or do you not know how great an evil despondency is?

C   Concerning the Isaurians, have no further fears, for they have returned to their own country. The governor has done everything about that, and we are abiding here in great security, much more so than when we were in Caesarea. For now I have no one to fear so much as the bishops—except for a few of them. But have no more fears about the Isaurians, for they have left, and when winter comes they will stay ensconced in their own homes. If they come out again, it will not be until after Pentecost.

D   And why are you saying that you are not enjoying [the benefit of] our letters? I have already sent you three long letters—one by the soldiers guarding me, another by Antony, and one by your servant Anatolius. Two of these letters especially were salutary remedies, sufficient to revive[5] anyone in despondency, anyone scandalized, and to lead them to complete restoration of spirit. When you receive them, go over them continually and thoroughly. You will perceive

[5]Literally, "rebuild."

their strength, you will experience their great healing power and benefit. Then you will inform us how much you have profited from them.

I have another one ready, similar to these, but I do not wish to send it now, because I am grieving greatly on account of your saying, "I am heaping up painful thoughts [*logismous*], even imagining things that do not exist." These words that you have uttered are unworthy of you, and because of them I redden with shame and hide my face. So read those letters, and you will no longer say these things, even if you insist on being despondent a thousand times over [*kan myriakis philoneikēs athymein*].

E   Tell me about the Bishop Heracleides,[6] for it is possible for him, if he wishes, to resign and escape from everything. There seems to be no other way. As for me, I have not arrived at anything grand, but I have made known to my lady Pentadia[7] that she [ought to] make great haste to find comfort in the midst of the evil.

You say that it is upon Bishop Heracleides' order that you dare to make known to me your distresses. What audacity this is! For I have not stopped saying, and I will not stop saying, that there is only one thing truly distressing, and that is sin. Everything else is dust and smoke. For what is grievous about being in prison and being bound with a chain? What is grievous about suffering wretchedly, when suffering wretchedly is the basis for such great gain? What is grievous about exile? What is grievous about the confiscation of one's property? For these words are empty of anything fearful; they are words empty of pain. And if you speak of death, you speak of a debt due to nature that everyone must submit to, even if no one [618] afflicts you. And if you speak of exile, you speak of nothing else but

[6]He was a deacon and friend of Chrysostom, whom he consecrated as bishop of Ephesus; he was condemned along with Chrysostom at the infamous Council of the Oak in 403.

[7]Pentadia was another one of the deaconesses connected to the Great Church in Constantinople. His three letters to her from his time in exile reveal his tender affection for her.

seeing [another] land and its many cities. And if you speak of the
confiscation of one's goods, you speak of liberty and being loosed
[from the burden of those things].

5.A Do not abandon Maruthas the bishop.[8] Look after him; take
care of him so as to draw him up from destruction. For I have
much need of him regarding affairs in Persia. Ascertain from him,
if you possibly can, what has been accomplished there through his
efforts since his return; and tell us if he has received the two letters
that we sent him. If he wishes to write to us, we will again write to
him. But if he does not want to, let him make known to Your Piety
what has happened there since his return, and what the prospects
are for accomplishments in the future. It is for this reason that I was
earnestly striving to be in communication with him. Let all this happen through your assistance, and fulfill your task, even if everyone
is rushing headlong to ruin. Your reward will be perfected. So by all
means make friends with him, as much as this is possible.

B I beseech you, do not run quickly over what I'm about to say
next, but consider it with great earnestness. The monks of Marsia
and Gothia,[9] among whom Bishop Serapion has been hiding, have
informed me that the deacon Moduarius has come, bringing word
that Unilas, that marvelous bishop whom I ordained not long ago
and sent to the Goths, has been laid to rest, after accomplishing
many great works. They also say that Moduarius brought a letter
from the king of the Goths, asking for a bishop to be sent to them.
Since I see no other way to turn the menacing catastrophe for the
good except for delay and postponement (for it is not possible for
them to sail into the Bosporus now, neither even toward that region
[of Gothia]), put the Goths off for a while, on account of the winter.

---

[8]A friend of Chrysostom, he was the bishop of Martyropolis in Persia, and held
an important place at the court of the Persian emperor.

[9]This was the name of the region north of the Black Sea, including the Crimean
Peninsula, in Chrysostom's time.

But do not skim over this lightly, for it is a very important matter to me.

There are two things that would especially upset me if they were to happen, which may God forbid!—if the [new] bishop is appointed by those working evil, contrary to justice, or if he is selected haphazardly. For they are not eager to select someone worthy. And if this happens—may it not happen!—you understand what will follow. Make haste, therefore, to do all you can to make sure that neither of these things happens. If it were possible for Moduarius to come to us silently, secretly, that would be a great thing. But if this is not possible, let what is possible under the current circumstances be done.

c   That which happens in monetary matters, and as occurred with the widow,[10] so it is also in worldly affairs. For just as she who gave her two mites surpassed those who gave more, because she was then [619] emptied of everything, so also with those who apply themselves to worldly concerns. For when they hasten to devote everything they have to fulfilling the work at hand, even if nothing results from it, they will still have their reward perfected.

I render many thanks to Bishop Hilarion,[11] for he wrote me asking that I allow him to go to his homeland and put everything in order, and then to return. Since his presence benefits me very much (for he is pious, a persevering man, and zealous), I urged him to depart and return quickly. Make sure that my letter is delivered to him securely, without getting lost; for with great desire and utmost yearning he has asked for letters from me, and his presence benefits me greatly.

So take great care with my letters. If the priest Helladios[12] is not there, make sure they are delivered to our friends by a trustworthy man who has a good head on his shoulders.

[10]Cf. Mk 12.41–44.

[11]We do not know where this bishop presided, but Palladius says that he was shamefully battered by the clergy hostile to St John, and exiled to Pontus (*Dialogue on the Life of Chrysostom* 20).

[12]A priest of Caesarea, a friend of Chrysostom.

From Cucusus, after
seven months in exile

End of 404

1.A When bodies struggle against fierce fevers, and seas fight savage [572]
winds, neither the bodies overcoming the ravages of the fever, nor the
seas subduing the disturbance caused by the gale, do so all at once, but
quietly, little by little. Bodies need additional time, after the fever has
left, to return to complete health, to be washed clean from the debility
lingering from the malady; while the waters, which continue to roil
and toss even after the winds cease, having been agitated by such a
great force, also need more time to return to perfect calm.

B It is not without forethought that I begin this letter to Your Piety
in this way, but for you to know that we are sending it to you by
necessity. For if we have destroyed the tyranny of your despondency
and demolished its stronghold through our previous letters, it is now
needful to take further care of you through these words, in order to
establish in you a profound peace, and having utterly blotted out
every memory of that disturbance, for you to show forth a luminous
and steadfast serenity, being secured in great joy.

C So this is what we are hastening to do: not only to banish your
despondency, but to fill you with great and continual gladness. This
is possible, if you are willing. For the immutable laws of nature do [573]
not make it impossible for us to force ourselves to make a change.
Rather, the power to manage our own welfare easily lies in the free

decisions of our will, and in this our joy resides. And you know this, as you remember from my frequent, long discourses (for not much time has elapsed in the meantime), in which I have expended myself in continually bringing forth examples from the history that I have been unfolding to you. For it is certainly not in the nature of things, but in the will of man, that our happiness naturally resides.

D   Because this is the way things are, there are many who are flooded with riches who do not consider this present life worth living; while there are many others, living in extreme poverty, who are more joyous than everyone else. And those who enjoy glory and honor and the protection of bodyguards often curse their life; while humble folk, born in obscurity, and virtually unknown, consider themselves to be more blessed than many others. All of this is because it is not in the nature of things, but in the will of man, that joy is found (for I will not cease chanting this refrain continually).

So do not disregard this, my sister, but stand up, and extend your hands to my words, and take advantage of our excellent assistance, so that we may set you completely free from the bitter bondage of your thoughts [*logismōn*]. If you are not willing to be zealous in this as much as we are, there is nothing else we can do for your healing.

And how would it be astonishing if things come to pass for us like this? For when our all-powerful God commands and counsels, and the one hearing does not obey what he says to do, the result can be nothing else but a great chastisement for the one who disobeys. Christ makes this clear when he says, "If I had not come and spoken to them, they would have had no sin; but now they have no excuse for their sins."[1] For this reason he himself laments for Jerusalem, saying, "O Jerusalem, Jerusalem, you who kill the prophets and stone those who are sent to you, how often have I desired to gather together your children, but you did not wish it. Behold, your house is left desolate to you."[2]

[1] Jn 15.22.
[2] Mt 23.37–38.

2.A Knowing this, my lady most beloved by God, take pains, and fight, and force yourself to cooperate with what I am saying—to repel, to chase away with the utmost ardor, the thoughts [*logismous*] troubling you, which are causing you such agitation, and such a storm. But, so that you might accomplish this, holding tightly to our exhortation, you must have no doubts.

And now it is necessary to prepare for you swords and lances, bows and arrows, and breastplates, shields, and leg-armor, in order for you to defend yourself, and to cast down and slaughter and leave for dead the troubling thoughts [*logismous*] that assail you. And where will we gather these weapons and projectiles for you, so that you might not only prevent your enemies from coming close, but that you might chase them very far away with much violence? From despondency itself, as we philosophize about it, making clear how heavy and oppressive a burden it is.

B   For despondency is for souls a grievous torture chamber, unspeakably painful, more fierce and bitter than every ferocity and torment. It imitates the poisonous worm that attacks not only the [574] body but also the soul, and not only the bones but also the mind. It is a continual executioner that not only tears in pieces one's torso but also mutilates the strength of one's soul. It is a continuous night, darkness with no light, a tempest, a gale, an unseen fever burning more powerfully than any flame, a war having no relief, a disease which casts a shadow over nearly everything visible. For even the sun and the air seem to be oppressive to those who are suffering from these things, and midday seems to be as darkest night.

C   Therefore the marvelous prophet says, to indicate this: "The sun set for them at midday."[3] He said this not because this heavenly body had actually disappeared, or had broken from its customary course, but because to the despondent soul the brightest moment of the day appears as night. For the darkness of night is not like the

[3] Am 8.9.

night of despair, which is not sustained by the order of nature, but is produced by the darkness of thoughts [*logismōn*] which are fearful and unbearable. Having a cruel visage, more savage than any tyrant, not yielding easily to anyone reaching out to destroy it, despondency often renders the soul it has seized harder than steel, when that soul is not much filled with wisdom.

3.A Why is it necessary to speak further on my own about this subject that I am developing, when we can come to victims near at hand, and learn from them all the power of this malady? If it seems good, let us go rather to another source to indicate this. For when Adam sinned that grievous sin which condemned, along with himself, the entire human race, he was condemned to distress. But there was one who committed a greater sin—a sin so much greater than Adam's that his might not even be accounted as a sin; for the Scripture says, "Adam was not deceived; but the woman, being deceived, fell into transgression."[4] This one, who was deceived and fell into transgression, and who thus prepared a potion [*pharmakon*] harmful to herself and to the man—she was condemned to a greater sorrow than being extended in strenuous toil; for as it says, "In your multiplying, I will multiply your sorrow [*lypas*] and your groaning; you will bear children in sorrows."[5] Not at all does he say in "pain," or "sweat," or "toil," but in "sorrow [*athymia*] and groaning." And this torture counterbalances a myriad of pains and deaths, and is much more grievous.

B   And what is worse than death? Does this not seem to be the chief of all the evils among men—fearful, unbearable, and seemingly worthy of a myriad of lamentations? But doesn't Paul say that the judgment of transgression is the most grievous thing? For to those who touch the sacred mysteries and take part in that fearsome banquet unworthily, such is the punishment they must undergo that

[4]1 Tim 2.14.
[5]Gen 3.16.

he says, "On this account many among you are weak and sick, and many are even falling asleep [in death]."[6]

c   Don't all the legislators condemn to this penalty [of death] those committing irreparable transgressions? And does not God lay down [575] in the law this most extreme punishment for those committing great sins? And was it not the fear of death that drove the patriarch [Abraham]—that one who later conquered nature itself[7]—to give his wife to the enjoyment of the barbarians, to the tyranny of the Egyptians, and to concoct that insolent scheme, and to beseech his wife to take part in that grievous, hypocritical tragedy of his? And neither did he blush with shame at giving the reason for the drama: "It will be," he said, "that when they see you brilliant in your youthfulness, and are seized by your beauty, they will kill me, and gain possession of you for themselves. Therefore, say that you are my sister, so that all will go well for me through you, and that I will live on account of you."[8]

d   Do you behold fear, do you behold trembling, seizing that exalted and philosophic soul? Do you see this adamantine one dissolving in agony? He lies about his parentage, he places upon his wife the role of another, making the lamb easy prey for the wolves. And regarding the thing that is the most unbearable for men—to see their wife insolently treated, or only having the suspicion of such—this [i.e., death] is more grievous than that. For here was not just the suspicion, but he was daring to make such violence [against his wife] possible. And he not only would have seen it, but he would have known that he had dared to make it possible, considering it something light and bearable. For this passion [the fear of death] subdued other passions, this most grievous affliction subdued other grievous afflictions, as the fear of death was triumphant over jealousy.

---

[6] 1 Cor 11.30.
[7] When he demonstrated his willingness to slay his own son at the Lord's command (Gen 22).
[8] Gen 12.12–13.

E   And the great Elijah, on account of this fear, became a runaway, a fugitive, a wanderer, fearing only the threat of one promiscuous and accursed woman. He who closed heaven[9] and accomplished other similar wonders could not bear the fear of her words; and agony so shook that heavenly soul that he suddenly abandoned his homeland and the people whom he had supported through many dangers. He undertook a journey of forty days all by himself, fleeing into the desert—after having demonstrated such boldness, such freedom of speech, and such courage.

F   It is the nature of death to be so exceedingly frightful. Every succeeding day it holds sway over our race, such that the appearance of someone dead suddenly terrifies each one of us, and throws us into confusion, and constricts us. Being watchful about the time [of our death] does not suffice to provide us consolation, even if we brace ourselves each day to behold it. And the sadness and stupor that it brings do not diminish with the passage of time, but are renewed and strengthened continually. And each day the fear comes again, undiluted, bursting forth afresh.

G   And this is very natural. For who is not chagrined and beaten down upon seeing one who just yesterday, and for many days, was walking, acting, bearing a myriad of cares—home, wife, children, servants, often placed at the head of entire cities, menacing, instilling fear, releasing from punishment and meting out punishments, [576] being occupied with a myriad of cares in the cities and in the countryside—suddenly becoming as silent as a stone? On account of whom a myriad of people are wailing, whose friends are broken-hearted, whose wife is broken in pieces, whose cheeks are withered, whose hair is disheveled, and around whom is gathered a choir of servants making much groaning, while he perceives nothing? With everything suddenly taken away—his thoughts, his mind, his soul, the bloom of his countenance, the movement of his members? And

[9]When he prayed that there be no rain for three years (1 Kg 17.1–7 [3 Kg, LXX]).

with the unpleasant things that follow—void of sound, void of feeling, the corruption, the pus, the worms, the ashes, the dust, the foul odor, the complete dissolution of the body, and all the bones pressed together in an ugly, misshapen way?

4.A But however debilitating this fear of death is, as shown forth above, and even in the experience of those saints I've mentioned, it is easier to bear than despondency. It is for this reason that I have extended myself in writing this "double course" of words, so that I may teach you that whatever price you pay, you will receive in its place a much greater corresponding recompense of good things. And so that you may learn that this is so, I will hasten to come to those who are crushed by despair, as I began to do earlier.

B   For Moses, the leader of the Hebrews, came announcing freedom [*eleutherian euangelizomenou*] and deliverance from the evils of the Egyptians, but they were not willing to listen to him, and the law-giver gave the reason: "Moses spoke to the people, but the people did not listen to Moses because of their faintheartedness [*athymousan*]."[10] And when with grave threats God threatened the Jews on account of their great lawlessness after their time of captivity—threats of exile, famine, pestilence, and cannibalism—he added this punishment, saying, "I will give them a despondent [*athymousan*] heart, failing eyes, and a soul melting away."[11]

But why is it necessary to speak of the Jews, a people without discipline, without knowledge, and enslaved to the flesh, not knowing how to philosophize, when it is possible to find an example even from among great and exalted men? For the choir of apostles had fellowship with Christ for three years; they were instructed much about immortality and other mysteries; they worked signs and wonders and miracles; for a long time they beheld Christ working miracles; they shared the intimacy of his table and his words; they

[10]Ex 6.9.
[11]Deut 28.53–65.

were instructed in every way. And yet, when they heard words that caused them distress, even though they had him continually with them, clinging to him like infants at the breast, so that they kept asking him constantly, "Where are you going?",[12] all of them were so overcome by the tyranny of despair and grief that they no longer asked him any questions. And Christ, in reproaching them for this, said to them, "You have heard that I am going to the one who sent me," and that I am coming to you, "and none of you asks me, 'Where are you going?' But because I have said these things to you, grief has filled your heart."[13] Do you see how the tyranny of despondency can darken love [erōta] and make men prisoners, and how it has done this?

c   To come back to Elijah—for I don't want to leave him as yet—after his flight and departure out of Palestine, he could not bear the tyranny of despondency [athymias], for he *was* greatly despairing [ēthymei], as the one who wrote the history made clear in saying, [577] "he departed to save his life."[14] Listen to what he said then, as he prayed: "It is enough now, O Lord; take my life from me, for I am no better than my fathers."[15] And that most fearsome thing [i.e., death], the height of torture, the chief of evils, the punishment for all sins, this he asks for in prayer, as he wishes to share in a portion of grace. For despondency is much more oppressive than death. In order to flee from the one, he takes refuge in the other.

5.A Here, I wish to resolve a certain question for you. For I know of your desire to have solutions for questions like this. What, therefore, is the question? If death is considered lighter to bear than despondency [athymias], why did Elijah abandon his fatherland and his people so that he might not be encompassed by death? And then, having fled from it, why does he now seek it?—so that you

[12]Jn 13.36.
[13]Jn 16.5–6.
[14]1 Kg 19.3.
[15]1 Kg 19.4.

may see how despair [*athymia*] is much more grievous than death. For when it was only the fear of death that was shaking him, it was natural for him to do everything he could to flee from it. But when despondency settled into him, and revealed its power in devouring, exhausting, and consuming him with its teeth, becoming unbearable to him, then what he formerly considered to be the heaviest burden of all [i.e., death], he now considers to be lighter than this [i.e., despondency]. So, too, Jonah, in fleeing from despair, sought refuge in death, saying, "Take my life from me, for it is better for me to die than to live."[16]

B   And David, whether he speaks on his own behalf, or whether he writes on behalf of others who are suffering the pains of despair, expresses the same thing: "For when the sinner stood against me, I was rendered mute and dumb; humiliated, I kept silent even about good things; and my grief was stirred anew. My heart burned hotly within me; and in my meditation, fire will be kindled."[17] He was indicating that that fire, fiercer than fire, is the passion of despondency. And in order to show that he could no longer bear its blows and pains, he says, "I have spoken with my tongue."[18] And tell me [O David], why are you saying this? He is begging for death, saying, "Make me to know my end, and the number of my days, so that I may know what I am lacking."[19] Using other words, he is indicating the same thoughts that Elijah expressed.

C   For while that one said, "I am no better than my fathers," this one hints at the same thing, saying, "Make known to me, O Lord, my end, so that I may know what I am lacking." Why am I being left on the earth, he is saying, and what am I lacking, and why am I living in this present life, while others have departed [from this life]? He is seeking death—whether he himself, or those for whom he is

[16]Jon 4.3.
[17]Ps 38.2–4, LXX.
[18]Ps 38.4.
[19]Ps 38.5.

speaking—and since it is not appearing, he desires to learn the time of its appearance: "Make me to know my end," in order to enjoy immense pleasure. Thus the fear [of death] becomes desirable on account of the unbearable pain of despair and the fire burning in his spirit: "For in my meditation fire will be kindled."

D   So then, expect great rewards for such torture—many prizes; [578] recompense beyond description; brilliant, abundantly blossoming crowns for such agony. For it is not only for the good one does, but also for the evil one suffers, that one obtains many rewards and great prizes. I am already proceeding to this powerful exhortation for you and for all those having need of it, to train them in patience, to instill courage, and not to leave in a weakened state those who are struggling against misfortunes.

6.A   That despondency is more grievous than all evils, that it is the height and head of fearful things, our discourse has already sufficiently demonstrated. Now it remains for us to tie together virtues and sufferings, so that you may learn clearly that it is not only for virtues, but also for sufferings, that there are rewards—even extremely great rewards—and for sufferings no less than for virtues. Indeed, this may be even more so for sufferings.

B   We bring forward now, if it seems good to you, that great athlete of patience, who shone brilliantly in various ways, that adamantine one, that rock, that one who appeared in the land of Ausitis,[20] who illuminated the world with the splendor of his virtue. And we will speak of his virtues and his sufferings, in order for you to see in which way he shone more brilliantly.

C   What, therefore, were his virtues? "My house," the scripture says, "was open to everyone coming to it, and it was a haven for all travelers."[21] All his goods virtually belonged to those in need.

[20]Job 1.1, LXX.
[21]Job 31.32.

"For I was," he says, "an eye for the blind and a foot for the lame. I was a father to the helpless, and I searched out the cause I did not know. I broke the molars of wrongdoers, and I plucked the spoil from the midst of their teeth."[22] "The helpless did not lack whatever they had need of, neither did anyone leave my door with an empty bosom."[23]

D   Do you see the differing expressions of his love for mankind [*philanthrōpia*], the various avenues of his almsgiving, and all the ways he gave assistance to those being wronged? Do you see him alleviating poverty, comforting widows, subduing those committing injustice, being formidable to those being abusive? For he not only demonstrated his zeal in assisting and giving aid (for many people do this), but he guided affairs to their end, with utmost vehemence: "I broke the molars of the wrongdoers," he says, in opposing with foresight their love of strife. He not only took a stand in his solicitude against the insolence of men, but also against the plots of nature, in redressing men's sins through his tremendous provision of assistance. Since he could not give them his own members—his eyes to the blind, his feet to the lame—he himself provided them with the use of his members, so that those who had lost their eyes, and those who had lost their legs, could see and walk, thanks to him. To what else could this love of his for mankind be compared?

E   You already know about his other virtues, so I will not make a long list of them in this discourse—his mildness, his gentleness, his wisdom [*sōphrosynēn*], his exactitude, and how vehement he was toward those committing injustice (something worthy of being marveled at); and how kindly and gentle he was, and sweeter than honey, [579] toward all others, and toward the people in his own house—who, in bringing forth proof of their great love [*erōtos*] for him, said, "Who will give us of his meat to satisfy us."[24] But if he was so yearned for,

22 Job 29.15–17.
23 Job 31.16, 34.
24 Job 31.31.

and so beloved, by those in his own household toward whom he sometimes had to be formidable, how much more was he beloved by all the rest of mankind?

7.A Therefore, having gathered these things together, and others more numerous besides, come walk with me to an enumeration of his sufferings, and we will see, by comparison, when he shone more brilliantly—when he accomplished those acts of virtue, or when he suffered the pains that caused him such great despair. When did Job shine forth more brilliantly?—when he opened his house to all those coming to it; or when, after it collapsed, he did not utter a bitter word, but honored God? For indeed, on one side was his virtue, and on the other side his suffering.

B   When was he more lustrous, tell me: when he offered sacrifice for his children and gathered them together in harmony; or when, after they had been buried, their lives having been destroyed in the most bitter way, he bore what happened with great wisdom [*philosophias*]? How did he shine forth more greatly?—when he warmed the shoulders of those who were naked with the wool from his sheep; or when, hearing that fire had fallen from heaven and had devoured his flock along with the shepherds, he was not shaken, neither was he troubled, but he bore what happened meekly?

C   When was he greater?—when his bodily health enabled him to stand up against the unrighteous, breaking the molars of the unjust, seizing their prey from the midst of their teeth, and becoming a haven for the oppressed; or when he saw this same body, the armor of the oppressed, now devoured by worms, with himself sitting on a dunghill, and, taking a piece of earthenware, scraping himself with it? "For I am wasting away as I scrape off clods of earth from the eruptions [from my sores],"[25] he says.

[25]Job 7.5.

So, on one side were all his virtues, and on the other side all his sufferings. But these latter declared him to be more illustrious than those. For this was the most bitter part of the battle, requiring the greater courage, the more well-stretched soul, the more philosophic mind, and having greater love for God.

D   On account of this, the devil, the one causing these events, shamelessly and very much like a pirate, retorted, "Is it not in vain that Job worships God?"[26] And when these things happened, Job departed, hiding himself, turning his back, without even providing a shadow of an insolent rebuttal. This is the summit of worthiness of a crown, this is the garland of virtue, this is the gleaming proof of courage, this is an effort of the highest degree of wisdom [*philosophia*].

E   This blessed Job, showing that the tyranny of despair is more grievous than death, called the latter a repose: "Death is a repose," he says, "for man."[27] And he asks him for a portion of grace in being delivered from the former, saying, "Would that God might grant that my prayer be answered, and that my hope be fulfilled. Would that he would make a beginning, and wound me, and draw me to my end. May the city be my grave, upon whose walls I have leapt."[28] [580] Thus despondency is more burdensome that everything else; and as it is more burdensome, its recompense will be greater.

8.A   In order that you may learn, from another angle, what the gain of sufferings is, even if one does not suffer for God—and no one would consider this to be an exaggeration—if one suffers and bears it nobly, and with meekness glorifies God for everything, he will be rewarded. Even Job did not know that he suffered those things for God—and indeed, this is why he was crowned, because he endured them nobly, not knowing the reason for his sufferings.

[26]Job 1.9.
[27]Job 3.23.
[28]Job 6.8–10.

B   And Lazarus,[29] encompassed with physical infirmity (and he also did not suffer for God), since he suffered very much, and persevered, and bore nobly the absence of anyone helping him, and the despondency caused by his wounds, by hunger, and by the contempt and cruelty of the rich man—you know how great the crowns are that he enjoyed. And yet we do not find any act of virtue attributed to him—not that he showed pity to the poor, or that he assisted the oppressed, or that he accomplished any similar good thing. We only hear of his sitting at the gate of the rich man, and of his infirmity, and of the tongues of the dogs, and of the contempt of the rich man towards him—that is, all the ways that he suffered so wretchedly. So even though he did not accomplish anything noble, and only because he bore his despondency nobly, he obtained the same end as the patriarch [Abraham] who did accomplish such acts of virtue.

C   After this, I would like to speak about something else that may seem paradoxical, but is true. If someone accomplishes a good thing, great and noble, but without having pain or danger or sufferings, his reward will not be very large. "For each one will receive his own reward according to his own toil"[30]—*not* according to the greatness of the virtue, but according to the weight of the suffering.[31] For this reason, Paul, when he boasted, did not boast only of the noble acts of virtue that he had done, but also of the evils that he had suffered. For after saying, "For they are ministers of Christ—I speak as a madman—but I more so,"[32] in emphasizing his superiority by way of comparison, he did not say, "I preached the gospel to such and such people," but rather, leaving aside his acts of virtue, he enumerated the evils that he had suffered, saying, "In toils more exceedingly abundant, in stripes beyond measure, in prisons more frequently, in danger of death often. Five times I received forty lashes save one from the Jews, three times I was beaten with rods, once I was stoned,

[29]Cf. Lk 16.19–31.
[30]1 Cor 3.8.
[31]Cf. 2 Cor 4.17.
[32]2 Cor 11.23.

three times I was shipwrecked, a night and a day I spent in the deep, in journeys often, in dangers from rivers, in dangers from thieves, in dangers from countrymen, in dangers from the Gentiles, in dangers in the city, in dangers in the country, in dangers in the sea, in dangers from false brethren, in weariness and toils, in sleeplessness often, in hunger and thirst and nakedness; and without speaking of the rest, the cares that I have each day."[33]

9.A Do you see this series of sufferings, and the occasion for his [581] boasting? Then he adds to these his works of virtue—but again, the sufferings have the greater importance, not the virtuous acts. For after saying, "the cares that I have each day," referring to the continual persecutions, disturbances, and difficulties (for this is what he means by "the cares"), he added, "the care for all the churches."[34] He did not say, "the correcting of," but "the care for," for this is more related to suffering than to virtue. And in what follows, likewise: "Who is weak," he says, "and I am not weak?" He did not say, "I am correcting," but "I am weak." And again, "Who is scandalized and I am not inflamed?"[35] He did not say, "I dissipated the scandal," but, "I took part in the sadness [*athymia*]." Then, indicating that these things especially bring a reward, he added, "If it is necessary for me to boast, I will boast in my weakness."[36] And he speaks next about his flight through the window in the wall, in a basket, for this was part of his suffering evils.

B If, therefore, sufferings have great rewards, and despair is the most grievous and most painful of all sufferings, imagine what will be the recompense for it! I will not cease chanting this refrain to you, in order to fulfill now what I promised in the beginning: to draw out from despondency itself the considerations that will give birth to consolation from despondency in you.

[33] 2 Cor 11.23–28.
[34] 2 Cor 11.28.
[35] 2 Cor 11.29.
[36] 2 Cor 11.30.

C   In order for you to learn from another angle how a virtuous act accompanied by pain is noble, and how doing that same act without pain has something lacking, Nebuchadnezzar, that Babylonian, living amid scepters and diadems, proclaimed a message of good news [*euangelikon*]. After the miracle of the furnace he announced the tidings [*kērygma*], not by speech only, but also by letters. And he wrote to all the world, saying, "Nebuchadnezzar, king over all peoples, tribes, and tongues, and those inhabiting all the earth, peace be to you in abundance! The signs and wonders which God the most high did upon me he is pleased for me to announce to you as great and mighty. His kingdom is an eternal kingdom, and his authority extends from generation to generation."[37] And he decreed by an edict that any people, tribe, or tongue who say a word against the God of Shadrach, Meshach, and Abednego will be put to death, and their house plundered. And he added, "For there is not another god who has power to rescue from danger in this way."[38] Do you see the threat in these letters? Do you see the fear? Do you see the instruction? Do you see this most excellent herald, and his letters addressed to all points of the earth?

D   What then, tell me? Did he receive the same recompense as the apostles, since like them he announced the news about the power of God, since with the same zeal as they he spread the message everywhere? No, not a great reward, but rather one very much inferior. Yes, he accomplished the same work as they did; but since pain was [582] not yoked with it, neither was suffering, therefore his recompense was diminished. For he acted with full authority, and without fear; while they were hindered, driven out, struck down, flogged, worn out with hard toil, thrown down headlong, cast into the sea, consumed by hunger, dying each day, weakened with every infirmity, and inflamed with indignation on behalf of each one being scandalized. Hence, the rewards for these pains and this despondency were

[37]Cf. Dan 4.34.
[38]Dan 3.96, LXX.

much greater. "For each one will receive his own wages," it says, "according to his own toil."³⁹ I will not stop saying this continually.

E   This is why God, the one who loves mankind [*ho philanthrōpos*], even when Paul besought him often to free him from sufferings and despondency and pains and dangers, did not assent: "On account of this I besought the Lord three times," he says, "but he did not grant my request."⁴⁰ Tell me, why was he about to receive such a great reward? Because he preached the gospel while living in luxury and festivity? Because he opened his mouth and moved his tongue while sitting at home? That would have been easy for anyone, even for one whose courage was failing, and who was living a soft and dissolute life. But now, for his wounds, for his enduring mortal dangers, for his journeys over land and sea, for despondency itself, for his tears and pains—"for three years," he says, "I did not cease night and day to warn each one of you with tears"⁴¹—he will receive, with great confidence, compensations and crowns.

10.A Therefore, meditating upon these things, and considering how great is the reward for a painful and toilsome life, rejoice and be glad, since from your youth you have trod a path full of a myriad of crowns, making profit through your continual and multitudinous sufferings. For bodily infirmity, in all its various forms, is more grievous than a myriad of deaths, since without ceasing it continually beleaguers you. Being showered with abuses and outrages; bearing calumnies against yourself without a pause; being overwhelmed with continual, extreme sadness; and having fountains of tears throughout all this time—each one of these trials is sufficient by itself to procure great advantage to those who endure such things patiently.

---

³⁹1 Cor 3.8.
⁴⁰2 Cor 12.8.
⁴¹Acts 20.31.

B   Lazarus, for his infirmity alone, partook of the same end as
the patriarch [Abraham];[42] and the publican, by the invective of
the Pharisee, acquired righteousness that far surpassed that of the
Pharisee;[43] and the chief of the apostles [Peter], by his tears, received
healing from the wound caused by that grievous sin [of denying
Christ].[44] Therefore, seeing that each of the sufferings that we've
mentioned—indeed, any one of them—seems to be sufficient, consider how great a reward you will receive, you who have endured all
your sufferings with tremendous patience throughout all this time.
For nothing, nothing makes someone so brilliant, so worthy of
emulation, so filled with a myriad of good things, as an abundance of
trials and dangers and pains and sadness, and being plotted against
continually—for those who, having no other expectations, bear
everything meekly.

C   Take the son of Jacob, for example: nothing rendered him
[Joseph] so blessed and esteemed as the calumny, the prison, the
[583] chains, and the misery that he suffered there. Great was the worth of
his discretion [*sōphrosynēs*] when he prevailed over the licentiousness of the Egyptian woman—when he eluded that wretched woman
who was inviting him to have illicit relations with her. Yet this was
not something as great as his sufferings. How is it praiseworthy,
tell me, not to commit adultery, not to undermine the marriage
of another, not to soil a couch that in no way belonged to him, in
order to avoid doing something unjust to his benefactor, and not to
cast disgrace upon the home of his protector? Rather, what made
him great was the danger, the machinations against him, the frenzy
of the captive woman [i.e., a captive of her passions], the violence
aimed against him, the inner chamber that the adulterous woman
had prepared for him like a prison without a way to escape, the nets
she stretched out everywhere for him, the accusation, the slander,

[42]Cf. Lk 16.19–31.
[43]Cf. Lk 18.9–14.
[44]Cf. Mk 14.72.

the prison, the chains, and the fact that after his great feat for which he deserved to be crowned, he was instead led into a dungeon, to be imprisoned with the worst sort of criminals—along with the filth, the irons, and all the misery of being in prison.

D   It is *then* that I see him more brilliant than when, seated on the throne of Egypt, he distributed grain to the needy, satisfying their hunger, and becoming a common haven for all. *Then* I see him shining, when his feet and hands are bound, more than when he wielded such power, wearing such glittering garments. For the way of life of the prison was like a marketplace for much spiritual gain for him. And while the luxury and comfort and great honor had much pleasure, it did not provide much gain.

Likewise, I do not count him blessed when he received honor from his father as much as when he was envied by his brothers, and had to live with them as enemies. For from his youth a cruel war was stirred up against him in his own home, even though those making war against him had nothing to reproach him for. But they were melting with envy, being torn asunder by it, since he was enjoying greater consideration from their father. So Moses the law-giver did not say that Joseph's favor had its origin in his virtue, but rather in the circumstances of his birth. For Jacob had begotten him after the others, in his extreme old age—children born in these circumstances are loved more, since they are born against all hope—and this is why he was so loved: "For the father loved him," he says, "since he was the son of his old age."[45]

11.A   These things the law-giver wrote, it seems to me, not to describe the reality, but to indicate the excuse and the pretext of the father. Seeing the lad being envied, and wishing to mollify this passion of his brothers, the father made up this reason for his [special] love [for Joseph], a reason that [he thought] would not much engender envy against the boy. That that was not the [real] reason for the boy's

---

[45]Gen 37.3.

[receiving special] favor, but rather the full flowering of the virtue of his soul, being more in full bloom than his age, is evident from Benjamin. For if it were on account of that former reason that Jacob loved Joseph especially much, it would have been imperative for him to love the younger one[46] more. For that one was born *after* Joseph, and so was even more a son of his old age.

But, as I've said, that reason was the fabrication of the father who desired to put an end to the brotherly warfare. But it did not succeed; rather, the flame burned exceedingly more. And since the brothers could do nothing at that point, they brought an evil accusation against him,[47] casting upon him a shameful charge, as they anticipated [i.e., acted in a way similar to] the foreign [Egyptian] [584] woman, revealing themselves to be worse than she. For she worked evil against a foreigner, while they did so against a brother.

B   And neither were they content with this evil, but added much more to it, by taking him alone into the desert, and sacrificing him, selling him, making him a slave instead of a free man—and in slavery of the worst kind. For they abandoned their brother not into the hands of people of his own race, but to barbarians, speaking a different tongue, and of a faraway, barbarian land. And God, in order to make him more illustrious, allowed what was happening with forbearance, while dangers succeeded dangers. For after their envy and their shameful calumny, they delivered Joseph to be sacrificed—into slavery more grievous than death.

C   Do not pass over lightly what I am saying, but imagine what it was like for this young man of a noble race, raised in his father's house with every freedom, and enjoying such great paternal love, to be suddenly betrayed by his brothers, yet having done nothing for which to be blamed; and to be delivered to barbarians speaking a

---

[46]I.e., Benjamin.

[47]Presumably St John has in mind here the brothers' indignant response to Joseph's dream, which they interpreted to mean that he would rule over them some day (Gen 37.5–8).

different tongue, having different customs, more like savage beasts than men; to be bereft of his country, exiled, made a servant of a foreigner instead of being a free citizen; and after having enjoyed such prosperity, to be cast down into the worst kind of slavery and misery, for which he was completely unaccustomed; and to be subject to the most cruel masters, and to be transported to a strange, barbarian land.

But the torments did not stop there; for again, plots followed plots against him, after the wondrous dreams that had predicted that his brothers would bow down to him. For the merchants who had received him did not keep him, but sold him to other barbarians who were even worse.

D   You can understand how important this discourse is about such disasters—having such masters in exchange for the former ones. For this rendered the slavery more difficult to endure, when those strangers who had bought him were crueler than the first ones. Now he was living in Egypt, that raging, God-resisting place—a place of shameful mouths and blaspheming tongues. He was living among Egyptians, one of whom was sufficient to turn the great Moses into a fugitive and an exile. And when Joseph had respite there for a short while, the man-loving God who does wonders, after having turned the savage beast who had bought him into a sheep, immediately prepared another arena for him—a stadium, and combats, and struggles, and sweating more abundant than before.

E   For the woman who owned him, regarding him with impure eyes, seized by the beauty of his visage, and conquered by the power of her passion, became a lioness instead of a woman through her unbridled desire. This new enemy lived in the same house as he, but he had other enemies as well. They drove him out of the house because they hated him, while she beheld the youth and burned with [585] lust for him. And so it was a double battle for him, or rather triple, and even more manifold than that. For he eluded the clutches of the one, but fell into the trap set by the others. And do not think that he bore this contest easily, for he endured it with much sweat.

12.A And if you wish to comprehend this clearly, consider that all of this was occurring in his youth—in the full bloom of his youth. This all beset him in the flower of his age, when the flame of natural desire rises most powerfully, when the storm of desire is great, when reason is at its weakest. For the souls of youths are not usually protected by much sound judgment, neither do they usually have great zeal for virtue. So on the one hand the surging of the passions is more violent, while on the other hand the reasoning power to govern the passions is weaker.

Besides his age and the force of nature, the licentiousness of the woman was great. And just as the hands of the Persians kindled the fire in Babylon with great zeal, stoking the fire with abundant fuel, throwing into the flames various combustible materials, in the same way that wretched, miserable woman kindled the flames of her furnace more cruelly, wafting perfumes, presenting herself alluringly, with painted eyes, seductive voice, affected movements and steps, soft garments, bedecked with gold, and with a myriad of other such machinations to bewitch the young man. And just as a skillful hunter takes in hand all the instruments of his art to ensnare his elusive prey, so that woman, knowing the chastity [*sōphrosynēn*] of the youth (for she was going to do this eventually), realized that she would have to prepare and employ every device of her licentiousness in order to take him captive. And even that did not suffice for her, for she chose a time and place favorable for the hunt.

B   For this reason she did not immediately launch her attack. Rather, she spent a long time in travail with her evil desire, preparing her plan, fearing that if she moved too quickly, and haphazardly, her prey would escape. One day, finding him alone in the house, performing his regular duties, she dug a deeper pit for him, unfurling to their fullest extent her wings of voluptuousness. Having the eagle nearly in her net, she went in, where it was only the two of them alone together. But she was not alone [in her scheming], for working together with her were his youthfulness, and the force of nature, and all her machinations; and she focused the full force of these things toward an unrighteous deed against that noble one.

What could have been more formidable than this temptation? Was this not fiercer than the furnace and the flame?[48]—this youth, stamped with a seal [of slavery], a slave, isolated, without a country, a stranger, an exile, under the authority of this licentious woman maddened with lust—a woman who was rich and surrounded with much power—and now he is totally isolated, for this is how she arranged things to make such a conquest; and she takes him, presses him to herself, flatters him, and leads him to her couch! And this, after all the other dangers and plots!

c   You know that most men, having been worn down and tired out by the difficulties [of life], if they were summoned to luxury and rest, to a soft and dissolute life, would run to it most enthusiasti- [586] cally. But not that one! For he lived in the midst of all of this, and yet he showed forth manly endurance and self-control. That chamber, which I dare to compare to the Babylonian furnace, and to the pit with Daniel and the lions, and to the belly of the beast of the sea which swallowed the prophet, was much more fearsome than any of the trials I've mentioned before. For in those trials the end result of the plot was the destruction of the body, while in this case, the end result would have been the complete ruin of the soul, and death unending, a calamity without any comfort. And this chamber was not only fearsome because of these things, but also because, along with her violence and craftiness, the woman was overflowing with flatteries, and with a fire, under many and various forms, that burns not the body, but devours the soul itself.

---

[48]Referring to the furnace that the three Hebrew youths were thrown into in Babylon.

D   And Solomon attests to this same thing, especially knowing with great accuracy how serious it is to have [unlawful] relations with a married woman: "Can anyone," he says, "receive fire into his bosom, and his garments not get burned? Can anyone walk upon fiery coals, and his feet not get scorched? Likewise, the one who lies with a married woman, and all who touch her, shall not be guiltless."[49] What he is saying is this: just as it is not possible for someone to be intimate with fire without getting burned, neither can one have relations with a woman and escape from the fire therein. And that which Joseph endured was much more fearsome. For while he did not touch her, he was in her power, alone, and threatened by her alone; and he had already been hard pressed by such evils, and had been worn down by such plots, while ardently desiring rest and security.

But in spite of all this, being almost within her grasp, and seeing a cunning beast advancing toward him, employing all kinds of weapons to slay him—physical contact, her voice, her eyes, her unguents, her cosmetics, her gold, her perfumes, her garments, her deportment, her words, the adornment of her surroundings, the solitude, the secrecy, her wealth and power, and having as her accomplices, as I've said already, his age, the force of nature, his slavery, being in a strange land—he conquered every one of the flames.

13.A More than the envy of his brothers, the hatred of his kinsfolk, the sale [into slavery], the power of the barbarians, the long exile, the sojourn in a foreign land, the prison, the chains, the long passage of time, and the wretchedness of the place—I assert that this temptation by that woman was more formidable than all of these things; for it involved the most extreme danger. And since he escaped from the war against him, the young man became as one wafted by a dewy breeze, through the grace of God and his own virtue. He was filled with such an untroubled and prudent [sōphrosynēs] spirit that he quickly put an end to the madness of that woman. And

[49]Prov 6.32–34, LXX.

since he came out unharmed, just like the youths in Persia escaped
from the flames—"for neither was there even an odor of fire upon [587]
them," it says[50]—he was shown forth to be a great athlete of chastity
[*sōphrosynēs*], comparable to steel.

B   Let us now behold what he experienced immediately after
the contest deserving of a crown—more plots, torments, mortal
dangers, slanders, unspeakable hatred. For that wretched woman,
moved by a fearsome madness, assuaged her love with anger, linking
passion to passion, adding unrighteous wrath to licentious desire;
and after being an adulteress, she became a murderer. Exhaling an
intense ferocity, and with murderous looks, she orchestrates a corrupt tribunal—Joseph's master, her own husband, the barbarian, the
Egyptian—and brings forth an accusation without witnesses. She
does not allow the accused to appear at the tribunal, but makes her
accusation quietly and confidently, taking advantage of the igno-
rance and good nature of the judge, and of her prestigious position
in the household, and of the fact that the accused is a slave. And
after asserting the opposite of what really happened, she prevailed
over the judge, persuading him to cast the vote that would assure
her of victory, thus condemning the guiltless one, pronouncing a
most grievous punishment—having him dragged away to prison
and chains.

Thus, having never seen the judge, this most marvelous man was
condemned. And what is even more grievous, he was condemned as
an adulterer, as one who lusted after his master's couch, as one who
undermined another's marriage, as one caught, as one convicted of
a crime.

C   There were the judge, the false accuser, along with the crowds
who did not know the truth, and the punishment that seemed to
make manifest the accuracy of the accusation—yet none of these
things shook him. And neither did he say, "Are these the rewards

[50]Dan 3.27.

for my dreams? Is this the end result [*telos*] of my visions? Are these
the prizes for my chastity [*sōphrosynēs*]?—a judgment contrary to
reason, a decree contrary to justice, and now, an evil reputation? Just
as I was formerly expelled out of my father's house, now I am led into
prison as an adulterer, as one who ruined the chastity [*sōphrosynēn*]
of a woman, and now everyone holds this judgment about me.

"And my brothers—those who were about to bow before me (for
this is what the dreams indicated)—are living in freedom, without
fears, in luxury, in their own country, in their father's house; while I,
who was about to be their master, am now bound together with grave-
robbers, and thieves, and purse slashers. And after being cast out of
my country, neither have I been delivered from troubles and annoy-
ances, but in a foreign land pits and swords are arranged for me once
again. And the one who orchestrated all this, who denounced me,
who deserves a double portion of justice for what she dared to do
against me, now dances and leaps as if she had been crowned with
trophies and brilliant garlands of victory, while I, who am in no way
guilty, suffer this extreme punishment."

D   No, he did not say any of these things; neither did he think them.
But as an athlete advances toward the crowns, just so he rejoiced
and was glad, not thinking anything evil against his brothers or the
adulteress. How do we know this? From what he himself said one
day to one of those bound together with him. He was so far from
being under the sway of despondency that he even dissipated the
[588] grief of others with him. For when he saw certain ones troubled and
confounded and despairing, he came to them immediately, asking
the reason. And learning that the disturbance was caused by visions
in dreams, he interpreted those dreams.

E   Then, he entreated them to remember him before the king, that
he might be delivered—if [they considered that] he was noble and
marvelous; and moreover, being human, that he would not want to
live miserably in those chains—so he asked them to remember him

before the king, and to persuade him to release him from his bonds. And when compelled to give them a reason why he had been thrown into prison, so that they could advocate for him, having a good word in his defense, he did not mention any of those who had done him wrong. Having loosed himself from the accusations brought against him, he was content with this alone, and did not name those who had mistreated him. He only said, "I was stolen fraudulently from the land of the Hebrews, without having done anything wrong, and they cast me into this pit."[51]

And why did you not mention the harlot, the adultery, the fratricides, the envy, the sale, the frenzy of the lady of the house, the attack, her licentiousness, the nets, her machinations, her flattery, the unjust judgment, the corrupt judge, the lawless sentence, the condemnation without a reason? Why did you keep silent about all these things, concealing them? "I chose not to remember these things as injuries," he says, "because for me they were crowns and rewards, and the basis for much profit."

14.A Do you see his philosophic soul? Do you see how he was cleansed from anger and higher than adversities? Do you see how he is sympathizing with the unrighteous, instead of remembering [their evil deeds]? For he did not bring an accusation against his brothers, neither against that drinker of blood. He only said, "I was stolen fraudulently from the land of the Hebrews, without having done anything wrong."[52] He did not mention a single person, neither the pit, neither the Ishmaelites, neither anything else.

But after these things, another unusual trial followed. For the one who had received such consolation, having been set free from his bonds, as Joseph had predicted, having been restored to his former position of honor, then forgot about his benefactor and the prayers of the just one. And so the minister was at the court of the king enjoying great prosperity, while the one who was shining more

[51]Gen 40.15.
[52]Ibid.

brilliantly than the sun with the bright rays of his virtue, still abode as a prisoner, and no one remembered him to the king.[53]

B   It was necessary for him to weave so many garlands for himself, and that there be greater rewards prepared for him. For this reason a double course, longer than usual, was imposed upon him. So it is that God allows arenas to remain, not to abandon anyone to the end, but to provide a way for those desiring so to excel in virtue—not to finish off the athlete, and neither to put the enemy of virtue out of the way. So he permitted Joseph to be thrown into the pit, and his garment to be dipped in blood; but he did not allow his life to be sacrificed. It was his brother who concocted this plan, but everything occurred according to the providence of God.

C   This also happened with the Egyptian woman. For what reason, [589]   tell me, did that hot-blooded, intemperate man (you know how the Egyptian race is easily incensed and prone to anger, for this passion is present in them to the extreme), believing Joseph to be a seducer, and that he had violated his own wife, yet did not do away with him, neither did he have him thrown into the fire? And why do you think this irrational man, who became so incensed upon the witness of only one party, who did not even allow the accused to say a word— why, at that moment of agony, did he demonstrate great good will [toward Joseph], even while beholding his wife in a frenzy, enraged, lamenting violently, wearing torn garments, whereby he was more inflamed than ever, weeping and groaning? And yet still he did not order him to be executed.

D   Why, tell me? Is it not evident that the one who bridles lions and cools the furnace, this one kept in check the measureless wrath of the beast, and calmed his inexpressible anger, so that he tempered the punishment proportionately? And one can see what this [providence] also produced in the prison, where God permitted Joseph

[53]Cf. Gen 40.23.

to be bound, to be with criminals, yet rescued him from the [usual] harshness of jailers. [E] You know how it is with jailers, yet Joseph's jailer was meek and gentle. And not only did he not make him undergo hard labor, but made him ruler over all those there[54]—and that, after Joseph had been received as an adulterer, as one condemned, as a notorious adulterer. And the jailer understood that the [alleged] act that was dared to be done did not occur in an ordinary house, but in one great and splendid. But this did not frighten him, or persuade him to be cruel to Joseph. So crowns for Joseph's sufferings were woven, for the aid [*symmachia*] of God was poured forth with great abundance.

F   I would wish to add more to the length of this letter, but I think that it has already surpassed its measure with great abundance. So now, in bringing my discourse to a close, I ask Your Piety, as I never cease asking, that you be far removed from despondency, glorifying God—which you have always done and are doing ceaselessly—rendering thanks to him for all these cruel and onerous things. In this way you will cultivate the most beautiful fruit, you will give a mortal wound to the devil, you will procure for us great consolation, with great ease you will make the cloud of despair vanish, and you will enjoy pure tranquillity. Do not become weakened, but rise up against that smoke—because, if you wish, you will dissipate all this despondency more easily than if it were smoke. And make this manifest to us through your letters, so that even from afar, we will reap the fruit [590] of great joy.

[54]Cf. Gen 39.21–23.

From Cucusus, after
eight months in exile

Beginning of 405

1.A Your tribulations have increased, the arena has become broader, [596] and the double course has become longer, as the anger of those plotting against you burns with a greater flame. But do not be troubled or shaken; rather, on account of these things, rejoice greatly and leap for joy—be crowned, and sing in chorus. If you had not previously inflicted a mortal wound upon the devil, that beast would not be more furious now than he was before. Surely this is proof of your courage and victory, and of his very great defeat—that now he attacks even more fiercely, exhibiting greater insolence, and pouring forth poison even more abundantly.

It's like the blessed Job, who, having suffered the loss of his goods and his children, proved that he could bear such cruel disasters graciously. And then the chief of evils rushed upon him—the besieging of his flesh, with the eruption of worms and a choir of wounds. I call it a *choir*, for it was all for him a crown, and a numberless host of rewards. But the devil did not stop with this, for since no other machination defeated him (and that disease was supposed to be the last of his afflictions), he brought upon him even more tribulations—arming his wife against him, irritating his friends, arousing his servants and making them like wild beasts, and exacerbating his wounds in all manner of ways.

B   But while even then the devil did not cease his attacks, they were turning upon his own head—just as your situation is becoming more brilliant, grander, and more radiant every day. Your riches are increasing, your merchandise is more abundant, your crowns are multiplying continually, your courage is greatly increasing through your sufferings, and the plots of your enemies are becoming a soothing balm, thanks to your patient endurance.

Such is the nature of tribulation: it renders those who bear it meekly and nobly to be superior to their sufferings, high above the devil's darts, teaching one to despise his plots. Trees nurtured too tenderly become weaker and less apt to bear fruit, while those which partake of changes in the air, receiving battering by the wind and heat from the sun's rays, stand stronger, full of leaves and laden with fruit—which usually happens with those growing by the sea.

Similarly, people who embark onto a boat for the first time, even if they are very courageous, from their lack of experience are agitated, and disturbed, and seized with dizziness and swooning; while [597] those who have voyaged much on the sea, and have endured many storms, and the deeps, and headlands, and crags, and attacks by sea creatures, and plots of pirates and brigands—and those who endure continual storms—abide on a boat more tranquilly than those who always walk on the land. And this is true not only for those sitting in the hull, but also for those sitting at the sides of the boat, and those standing fearlessly at the bow and at the stern. And those sailors who at first sat still, beholding everything with trembling and fear, after experiencing many storms, are pulling ropes, hoisting sails, seizing oars, and running around everywhere on the boat with ease and lightness.

C   Therefore do not be troubled by what befalls you. Our enemies have actually strengthened us, as they are not able to make us suffer; and having shot all their arrows, neither have they been able to put us to shame, or make us a laughingstock. And all enemies throughout the world are revealed to be this way everywhere.

These are the wages of those who hatch plots; this is the end result [*telos*] of wars. Ah! What a great thing virtue is, as well as disdain for present affairs! Through plots, virtue makes her profit; through those conspiring against us, she is crowned; through those doing evil, she shines more brightly; through those endeavoring to do mischief, she makes stronger the one following her, and more exalted, and unconquered, and impregnable—and all this without weapons. For not having need of lances, or ramparts, or trenches, or towers, or materiel, or armies—but only with firm thinking, and an immovable soul—she confounds every human machination.

2.A Therefore, singing these things, my lady most beloved by God, both to yourself and to those fighting the good fight with you, elevate your thinking, and arrange your army in battle array; for the crown of your virtue becomes double, and triple, and even more manifold through your sufferings—and through the encouragement that you've given others in these things, persuading them to bear all things meekly, to disdain the shadows, to despise the falsity of dreams, to trample upon the mire, to consider the smoke to be of no account, to refuse to reckon the spiders' webs to be annoying, and to skip over the moldering grass. For all of these things indicate the vanity of human happiness, which is so paltry compared with virtue.

One cannot easily find an image that exactly depicts this vanity. Moreover, for those aspiring to it—those who suppose that it will bring them pleasure in these days—this nothingness is not a small wound to bear, not only in the future age, but also in the present life. For just as virtue, at the moment at which it enters the war, leaps for joy and blooms and appears more brilliant, so evil, at the moment at which it is paid attention to and flattered, reveals its weakness, its great absurdity, and its comedy.

B What is more pitiable, tell me, than Cain at the moment at which he appears to have overpowered and vanquished his brother, [598] being borne about by his anger and wrath which produced that loathsome deed of injustice? What is more impure than that hand that appeared to have triumphed, that hand with which he delivered the blow and committed the murder? What is more miserable than that shameful tongue that ordered the deception and set the traps? And why should I mention all the members of his body that contributed to the murder? For his entire body was punished, when he was condemned to a life of continual groaning and trembling.

O new thing! O paradoxical victory! O strange trophy! For the one slain and lying dead is crowned and proclaimed, while the one who was victorious and triumphant not only goes uncrowned, but because of his "victory" is punished, subjected to unbearable torment and ceaseless anguish. The one who was struck, who is dead and without a voice, accuses the one moving around, who lives and speaks. And it is not actually the body of the dead one doing this; but his mere blood alone, separated from his body, is sufficient to make the accusation.[1]

Such is the superiority of virtuous men, even when they are dead; and such is the wretchedness of evil men, even when they are alive. If in the arena the prizes are so great, imagine the greatness of the rewards at the time [kairos] of recompense, in the distribution of those good things that surpass speech. For the painful things that are brought upon us by men resemble, in their paltriness, those who confer them. But gifts and rewards are bestowed by God, through his ineffable generosity.

c   Rejoice, therefore, and be glad; be crowned, lead a procession; trample upon the goads of your enemies, more than others who tread upon mire. And declare to us ceaselessly news of your welfare, so that in this we may overflow with great joy. For you know that it will give us not a little comfort, as we sit in this solitude, when we learn continually of your increasing strength. Be strong!

[1]Cf. Gen 4.10; Heb 12.24.

From Cucusus, after about ten months in exile

Spring, 405

1.A It is after having mounted up from the very gates of death that I [598] am writing to Your Moderation [*kosmiotēta*]. Therefore I am rejoicing greatly that your servants have come to see us now, while we are "anchored in port." For if they had arrived while I was still being tossed on the sea, suffering from the dreadful waves of my illness, it would not have been easy for me to deceive Your Piety through sending you good news instead of bad. Indeed, the winter was much more grievous for us than usual, rendering the distress of my stomach worse.

I spent these past two months no better than dead—yea, even worse than dead. I was surviving just enough to perceive the terrible things encircling me everywhere. All was night to me—the day, the dawn, the height of noonday—and I spent the whole time nailed to my bed. I tried a myriad of ways to alleviate the wound caused by the cold, but they all failed. When I kindled a fire, I had to endure [599] the most grievous smoke; and when I enclosed myself in one little room, having a myriad of blankets, and not daring to set foot over the threshold, I suffered the most extreme torments—continual vomiting, headaches, lack of appetite, and constant sleeplessness. I spent the whole time as if it were a vast sea of night.

But that I might not distress your mind by dwelling upon more of those difficulties, we are now delivered from all these things. For

131

as soon as spring approached, bringing a certain small change in the air, everything vanished on its own. But I still need to take many precautions regarding my diet; therefore I only give my stomach light nourishment, which it can easily digest.

B   It was not just by chance that it was brought to our attention, and that we learned fully, that Your Moderation was brought nearly to your last breath. And because we cherish [*stergein*] you greatly, being concerned and anxious about your affairs, we were overjoyed to be delivered from these cares even before your letters arrived; for many people came from there [i.e., Constantinople] announcing everything concerning your health.

So now I rejoice greatly and am glad, not only for your deliverance from illness, but more than everything, for the way you nobly bore everything that befell you, calling all of those things an idle tale—and for something even greater: that you applied the same name to your bodily illness, which reflects a youthful soul and one brimming with the fruit of courage. For not only enduring difficulties nobly, but also being insensible to them, disdaining them, and with great freedom from cares being wreathed with the crown of patience—without being wearied, without sweating, without having anxiety, and without causing others to be anxious, but as one leaping for joy and dancing—all of this is proof of a most excellent philosophy.

Therefore I rejoice and leap for joy, I flutter with delight, not even noticing my present isolation or its difficult conditions, but being happy and radiant, and greatly glorying in the grandeur of your soul and your repeated victories—and not only for your sake, but also for the sake of that great and very populous city, for which you are a tower, a haven, a rampart, a brilliant voice for rising above worldly cares, teaching both sexes through your sufferings to strip readily for such battles, and to descend into the arena with all courage, and to endure easily all the sweat of these contests.

C   And the wonder is that without entering into the marketplace [*agoran*] or appearing in the midst of the city, but staying at home, sitting in a narrow inner chamber, you anoint the combatants—with the sea raging and the waves cresting; with headlands, and deeps, and crags, and fierce sea creatures appearing everywhere; and profound darkness encompassing everything. But you are sailing as if at midday, with calm seas, and with the wind wafting from behind the ship. Unfurling the sails of patience, you sail on with great ease, [600] not only without being overwhelmed by this fierce storm, but also without even being sprinkled by the spray.

This is exceedingly natural; for such is the power of virtue—like rudders. For merchants, and pilots, and sailors, and navigators, when they behold a gathering of clouds, or an inrushing of fierce winds, or the crashing of waves with the most exceedingly seething foam, they keep their boats inside the harbor. And if it happens that they are tempest-tossed on the open sea, they do everything to devise a way to put their vessel to anchor in a harbor, or near an island or a promontory.

But you, in the midst of a myriad of winds, with wild waves crashing upon one another, and the depths of the sea heaved up by the exceeding fierceness of the storm, with some people being submerged, others floating dead upon the waters, and still others naked and being borne on planks—you are abounding in the midst of this ocean of evils, calling all these things but idle tales, and sailing prosperously in the midst of the storm.

And all this is exceedingly natural. Pilots, even if they are a thousand times wise in their art, still do not have skill sufficient to withstand every kind of storm. This is why they often flee from doing battle against the waves. [D] But you—your art is higher than every storm; and the power of your philosophic soul is stronger than a myriad of armies, more powerful than weapons, more secure than towers and ramparts. Soldiers have weapons, and ramparts, and towers that are useful only for the security of the body, but not always, and not in every way; for there are times when all these things are insufficient, and leave destitute of protection those who rely on them.

Your weapons do not confound barbarian arrows, or the war engines of men, or any attacks and ruses of that kind; rather, they have trampled upon the exigencies of nature, destroying their tyranny and leveling their fortress. In fighting constantly against demons, you have won a myriad of victories, without having received a single blow, standing unwounded in the midst of a hail of arrows, and throwing the spears thrown at you back again upon those who hurled them.

Such is the wisdom of your art: through the evils that you suffer, you repay those bringing them upon you; and through their plots, you bring to grief those making war against you. And so the evil becomes the starting place, the foundation, for greater glory for you.

Knowing these things well, and having gained perception through experience, you naturally call all these things an idle tale. And how should you not call them an idle tale, tell me, when having received a mortal body, you despise death like those hastening to leave a foreign country to return to their own fatherland? You are living with a most grievous infirmity, and yet you are more cheerful than those who are thriving physically and swelling with pride. And you are not being worn down by insults, or being puffed up with honors and glory—which have been the cause of a myriad of evils, even for many in the priesthood who were brilliant, who had reached great old age, who were extremely venerable, and yet they suddenly slipped and lay exposed as a common spectacle for those wishing to ridicule them.

But you, a woman encompassed with a body as frail as a spider's web, and receiving such attacks—not only have you not suffered [601] such a fall, but you have also prevented many others from falling. There are many who go forward into battle; but from the beginning, from the very starting gate, so to speak, they are defeated. And you, who have circled the last post a myriad of times, and have in each race seized the prize—you have shone forth as an example in various kinds of contests and struggles. And this is entirely natural: for in contests of virtue, neither one's age nor one's body matters, but only one's spirit and purpose. Thus women have been crowned, and men have been thrown down; thus children have been proclaimed victors, and old men have been covered with shame.

E   It is always needful to admire those who pursue virtue—but especially when a great number abandon it, when one can scarcely find anyone laying hold of it. On account of this, it is completely fitting to marvel at your grace [*emmeleian*], when so many men, women, old men, those seeming to have great recognition, are turning away and falling prostrate before the eyes of all—and this, not due to the great intensity of the warfare, or from the fearsomeness of the enemy's battle array; but they are falling down even before the attack, being defeated even before the struggle. While you—*after* such battles and onslaughts—not only have not weakened, neither have you been troubled by the flood of evils; but you are all the more vigorous, and the increase of struggles provides an increase to your strength. So the memory of your virtuous deeds can become the basis for your cheerfulness and joy, and greater zeal.

Therefore we rejoice, we leap for joy, we are filled with gladness. And I will not cease saying this continually and carrying everywhere the basis of my joy. And if our separation grieves you, your virtues should be a great consolation for you. As for us, even though we are banished to such a great distance, in speaking of your courage we reap the fruit of not a little gladness.

From Cucusus, after about twelve months in exile

Summer, 405

1.A What do you say? Have you not stood for a trophy? Have you not [601] carried off a brilliant victory? Have you not put on an ever-flowering crown?[1] Is it not the case that in all the world, everywhere on earth, they are singing of your virtuous deeds? While your exploits, your struggles, have occurred in one particular place, and while in running your double-course in this specific arena you have been covered with blood instead of sweat, nevertheless the glory of these things and their fame have reached the ends of the inhabited earth.

Yet you, desiring to accomplish even greater things, and to gain more abundant prizes, have added to these things crowns of humility, in saying that these are as different from the other crowns as the dead are from the living. That these are the words of humility, we will endeavor to convince you from the things that have happened themselves. For you have been expelled from your country, your home, your friends, your relatives; you have withstood exile; you have not ceased mourning every day; and you have completed what was lacking in your nature through the abundance of your good intentions. For while it is not possible for anyone to experience death many times, yet you have done so in your thoughts. And what is grander still: in enduring your sufferings, and in expectation of [602] other trials besides, you have not ceased agreeing with God in these

---

[1]In Chrysostom's day, the crowns bestowed on victors in athletic contests were circular garlands woven of flowers.

things—offering glory[2] to him for these things, and especially for giving the devil a mortal wound. And that he did receive a mortal wound is evident by how much he then prepared for further warfare, which is why the more recent events have been more grievous than what happened previously.

B   For just as a scorpion or a snake, upon receiving a devastating blow, fully draws out its sting to send it forth against its attacker, making evident its pain-filled fury directed against the one giving the blow, so also that insolent beast, since he received deep wounds through your marvelous and exalted soul, sprang forward to a greater extent, and brought forth more trials. For it is he who brought the trials, and not God; but God permitted this in order to increase your riches, to make greater your gain, to procure for you greater rewards and a more abundant recompense. Therefore, do not be shaken, do not be troubled.

Who has ever tired of riches? Who has ever been disturbed upon coming to the most exalted heights? If those who gather human good things which are perishable, more fleeting than a shadow or than flowers that are rotting, or rather withering away, still leap for joy, and dance, and flutter with a pleasure that appears but then quickly disappears, in imitation of the course of a surging stream, how much more is it right for you to rejoice! For even if you were overwhelmed at first by despondency, the present circumstances afford you the occasion for the greatest joy! For the treasure that you have gathered for yourself is inviolable. And the worthiness that has been forged through these sufferings of yours does not know, nor does it have, an end; for it is limitless, and cannot be cut short by difficult circumstances, or by the plots of men, or by the assaults of demons, or by death itself.

C   If you wish to weep, weep for those who are doing such things— those instigating these evils, and their accomplices, who all have

---

[2]Literally, "a doxology"—*doxologian.*

gathered up for themselves the greatest punishment in the future, who have already inflicted upon themselves the final judgment; while those turning away from them consider them to be enemies, cursed and condemned. And if they do not realize these things, they are because of this most especially to be pitied, most worthy of tears.

For they are just like those possessed with mental illness—who kick and strike those who approach them, randomly and vainly, even often those who are their benefactors and friends, not recognizing the mania that possesses them. Therefore their illness is incurable, for neither do they allow doctors to approach, nor do they take medicine; but rather they treat in a contrary way those who wish to heal and benefit them.

So this is why they are most to be pitied, for they do not recognize their wickedness. And if they do not amend themselves when they are condemned by others, yet they cannot escape from the irresistible judgment of their own conscience. For this is unavoidable, and unbribeable; it does not accede to any fear, or any flattery; it is not deadened when given gifts; and it is not withered by the long passage of time.

2.A Jacob's son, the one who told his father that an evil beast had devoured Joseph, in playing out this evil drama, and undertaking [603] through this mask to shade over completely the [supposed] death of their brother, deceived his father—but not his conscience, which gave him no rest. Rather, it continued to tear him in pieces, ceaselessly crying out, never closing its mouth.

After a long period of time, the one who denied having dared to do the audacious deed—who had not confessed to any man, neither had anyone accused him, or blamed him, or attacked him, neither did anything happen to remind him of that dramatic scene—when his freedom and his very life were threatened, it was revealed that the judgment of his conscience had indeed never stopped crying out even over so long a period of time, neither had it been checked. For he said these words: "Truly we have sinned regarding our brother;

for when he besought us, we despised his anguish and the pain of his soul. And now his blood is demanding an account of us."[3]

B   However, there was another accusation directed against him, condemning him as a thief; for as one stealing a little golden cup, he was brought to the judgment seat. But since he had done nothing to warrant reproach, he did not grieve about it.[4] Yet neither did he say that he was suffering on account of what he was indeed condemned for, which led him into bonds.[5]

But no one reproached him for that, neither did anyone demand an account, neither did anyone drag him before the tribunal. Rather, since no one reproached him for what he had dared to do, he became his own accuser and judge. His conscience seized him; and this one who shed the blood of his brother with such shamelessness and who suffered nothing for it, now became sympathetic to his brother's suffering, and accused the whole band of his accomplices of blood-guiltiness, showing forth the cruelty of the tragedy in saying, "When he besought us, we despised his anguish and the pain of his soul." "For nature ought to have sufficed," he is saying, "to soften us and incline us to pity. But Joseph added his tears, and supplications, and still he did not move us," for "we despised his anguish and the pain of his soul." "This is why this court of justice has been formed for us," he is saying; "this is why we are in danger of blood, since we have sinned against his blood."

C   Likewise, Judas, not bearing the condemnation of his conscience, ran and took a rope and destroyed his life by hanging himself. But after he dared to make that shameless contract, saying, "What would you like to give me, if I hand him over to you?"[6] he did

[3]Gen. 42:21.

[4]Cf. Gen 44. Joseph hid a small silver cup in his brother Benjamin's sack and then accused all his brothers of theft.

[5]That is, into the bonds of his conscience, which was tormenting him for what he previously had done to Joseph.

[6]Mt 26.15.

not blush in front of the others upon hearing that one of the disciples would stir up trouble against their teacher, and neither in the days that followed was he pricked at heart. Rather, he was drunk with the pleasure that his love of money brought him. And neither did he perceive the condemnation of his conscience very much.

But after he committed the sin and received the silver, then the pleasure of his gain stopped; and the reproach of the sin suddenly flared up, even though no one obliged him, no one forced him, no one exhorted him. Rather, he went on his own to those who had given him the money, and threw it down, and confessed his sin, saying to those listening, "I have sinned in betraying innocent blood."[7] For he did not bear the condemnation of his conscience.

And this is the way of sin. For before one commits a sin, it makes [604] the one it has captured drunk. But when its purpose is fulfilled and it is committed, then its pleasure vanishes and is extinguished; the sinner then stands naked and condemned, and his conscience plays the role of the public executioner. Tearing into pieces the one who has sinned, it demands the most extreme punishment, weighing him down more heavily than all the lead in the world.

3.A Such are the tortures endured in this life. As to those in the next life, you know what evils are stored up then for those committing such great crimes. It is necessary, therefore, to weep for them, to lament for them—even as Paul also did, who, in rejoicing with those who struggle and fight and suffer evils, also bewailed those sinning. Therefore he said, "lest when I come, my God will humble me before you, and I shall bewail many of those who have sinned but have not repented for the uncleanness and impurity which they have practiced."[8] But to those who fight, he says: "I rejoice and congratulate all of you."[9]

[7]Mt 27.4.
[8]2 Cor 12.21.
[9]Phil 2.17.

Therefore let nothing trouble you—neither anything that happens, nor anything that threatens to happen. For the waves do not violently shake the rock; rather, the more forcefully they dash upon it, the more they become dissipated. This is the way things work for the one standing firm; and indeed, there is a greater advantage. For the waves do not shake the rock; and they not only have not shaken you, but they have made you stronger. Such is wickedness, and such is virtue. The one, when attacked, is destroyed; while the other, when attacked, shines more brilliantly. And this one receives prizes not only after the contests are over, but even in the midst of them; for the struggle for virtue itself brings its own recompense. But when the other prevails, then it especially is put to shame, then it is punished, then it is filled with much dishonor; and even before the punishment that is reserved for it, it receives retribution even as it acts, and not only afterwards.

B If this discourse is not clear enough, listen to the blessed Paul distinguishing between the two. For in writing to the Romans, denouncing the impure life of some of them, he indicates that before the punishment, even in the midst of the sinful activity itself, the sin has its corresponding punishment. Having recalled the lawless intercourse of women and men that transgressed the bounds of nature, being conceived through a certain strange desire, he says this: "For their women exchanged the natural use for what is against nature. Likewise also the men, abandoning the natural use of the female, burned in their lust for one another, men with men working what is shameful, and receiving in themselves the fitting recompense of their error."[10]

What are you saying, O Paul? Is it not without doubt that those daring to commit this lawless intercourse do so under the influence of their desire? How, therefore, do you say that they are punished even in the midst of their action? He is saying, "I base my judgment not on the pleasure of those who are diseased, but on the nature

[10]Rom 1:26–27.

of the actions themselves." For concerning adultery, even before [605] its final punishment, the adulterer is punished in the midst of the adulterous act, even if he seems to find pleasure as he makes his soul worse, and more vile. The man-slayer, too, even before he sees the tribunal and the sharpened swords, and before he gives an account of the things he has dared to do, puts *himself* to death in committing murder—again, rendering his own soul more vile.

As disease is for the body, and as fever is for dropsy or some other such thing, and as rust is for iron, and the moth is for wool, and the worm is for wood, so is wickedness for the soul. For it reduces a free man to slavery, and to slavishness. Why do I say "reduces to slavery, and to slavishness"? Because it renders the soul to be without reason, like the animals—turning one into a wolf, another into a dog, another into a serpent, another into a viper, and another into some other kind of beast.

c   The prophets show this forth, making evident the complete transformation which wickedness can effect in a person; as one of them said, "Mute dogs who cannot bark,"[11] thus comparing with enraged dogs those who are rotten among men, who make plots stealthily. For it is not with barking that such dogs attack; but they approach in silence, and inflict greater wounds upon those they catch than barking dogs do. And again, another prophet called a certain man a crow. And another said, "A man being in honor did not understand; he was compared to senseless cattle, and became like them."[12] And the greatest of the prophets [St John the Baptist], the son of a barren woman, as he stood by the Jordan, called certain men "serpents and a brood of vipers."[13] What can be equal to this punishment, when someone made in the image of God, enjoying such honor, endowed with reason and a most gentle [*ēmerōtaton*][14] way of life, catapults himself into such savagery?

[11]Is 56.10.
[12]Ps 49.13, 21 (48.13, 21, LXX).
[13]Mt 3.7.
[14]Literally, "tamed."

4.A Do you see how wickedness, even before the final punishment, brings its own torture in itself? And learn also how virtue, even before its final recompense, brings its own recompense in itself. Just as with the body—and nothing prevents our use of this example that brings much clarity—just as, therefore, with the body, when it is in good health and feeling well, when it is free from all disease, even before it experiences the full enjoyment of healthfulness it gains a taste of the pleasure of health; and neither adverse weather, nor drought, nor cold, nor a sparse table, nor any other such thing is able to cause it sorrow, for its health is sufficient to drive away any harm arising from such trials—things which customarily agitate the soul. This is why Paul—whipped, beaten, suffering a multitude of tortures—rejoiced in saying, "I rejoice in my sufferings on your behalf."[15] For it is not only in the kingdom of heaven that the reward for virtue is laid up, but even in the midst of suffering. And the greatest reward is to suffer for the truth.[16]

Therefore the choir of apostles left the council of the Jews rejoicing, not only on account of the kingdom of heaven, but for having been judged worthy of being dishonored on behalf of the name of [606] Jesus.[17] For this is in itself a great honor, a crown, a prize, and the basis of unfading pleasure.

B Rejoice, therefore, and leap for joy. For it is not a small contest, but a very great one, to be the object of slander—and especially when it is such a grave accusation that is brought before the public tribunal against us—that of arson![18] This is why Solomon, wishing to indicate how severe this contest is, stated: "I have seen calumnies under the sun, and I see the tears of those being slandered, and there is no one

---

[15]Col 1.24.
[16]Cf. Mt 5.10–12.
[17]Acts 5.41.
[18]St Olympia and other followers of St John were accused of starting the fire that burned down the cathedral and other public buildings in Constantinople during the night when John was led into exile.

to comfort them."[19] If the struggle is great—as this one surely is!—it is evident that the crown laid up for it is greater.

This is why Christ commands those who are fighting this battle with befitting patience to rejoice and leap for joy: "Rejoice," he says, "and leap for joy, whenever anyone speaks an evil word against you for my sake, for great is your reward in heaven."[20] Do you see how much pleasure, how much recompense, how much happiness our enemies have become the cause of for us? How, therefore, would it not be marvelous that those evils which they were not able to work against you are rather turned into the opposite, which you arranged by yourself? And what is this I'm saying? That they were not only *not* able to demand punishment of you, but they provided you with a source of happiness, the basis of unfading pleasure.

C   But you, torturing yourself with despondency, are demanding a punishment of yourself, being thrown into disorder, being shaken, being filled with much chagrin. This is just what *they* should be doing—if they should ever desire to recognize their own evil-doing. They are the ones who ought to be sorrowing now, weeping, sinking, hiding themselves, burying themselves, neither looking at the sun, but enclosing themselves in shadow, lamenting for their own evils with which they have encompassed so many churches. In contrast, it is needful for you to rejoice exceedingly, to exult, since you have attained the summit of virtues.

D   You know, you know very well, that nothing is equal to patience; for this is most especially the queen of virtues, the foundation of right actions, the port without waves, peace in the midst of war, calm in the midst of billows, security in the midst of plots, rendering the one who has attained it to be stronger than steel. And neither brandished weapons, nor drawn up battle lines, nor gathered engines of war, nor deployed bows and spears, nor the army of the demons

[19]Eccl 4.1.
[20]Mt 5.11–12.

itself, nor the fearful phalanxes of the opposing powers, nor even the devil himself, with all his armies and engines of war, are able to cause you damage.

What, therefore, are you afraid of? What are you troubled about, when you are working yourself up to despise even life itself, should that moment come? But do you desire to see the dissolution of the [607] evils that afflict you? This will come—yes, it will come quickly, as God permits.

Rejoice, therefore, and exult, and revel in your virtues. And by no means ever give up hope that we will see each other again; and may we remind you of this through these words.

From Cucusus, after about fourteen months in exile

Late summer, 405

1.A In two ways we behold God's ineffable love for mankind—first, [620] that he permitted you to be afflicted with such trials, one after another, which succeeded in producing for you such brilliant crowns; and then, that he delivered you quickly from them, so that you would not be stretched for too long by the evils afflicting you. This is how God generally governs the affairs of men, as we can see from the lives of the apostles and prophets; for sometimes he allows the waves to rise up, and at other times he takes command over an ocean of evils, and after the frightful storm he establishes a luminous calm.

Cease, therefore, your crying, and stop torturing yourself with grief. And do not look only upon the torments that have been afflicting you ceaselessly one after another, but also consider the swiftness with which you have been freed from them, and the ineffable reward and recompense that they bring.

B Whatever is like a spider's web, or shadow, or smoke, or anything else even more paltry—this is what the fierce torments coming upon you are like in comparison with the prizes that will be given to you in the coming age. For what is it to be driven out from one's city, to be transferred from place to place, to be harassed everywhere, to have one's goods confiscated, to be dragged before the tribunal,

147

to be savagely mistreated by soldiers, to endure the opposition of those who have received from you a myriad of benefactions, to be abusively treated by both servants and free men, when the prize for all these things is heaven, along with those pure, good things which are impossible to describe and which have no bounds, and the enjoy-
[621] ment of which will be eternal for those who have procured them?

Therefore, leave off considering the plots, the insults, the loss of your possessions, being continually uprooted, and living in a foreign country; and trampling upon all these things as if they were more paltry than mud, think rather about the treasures that are laid up for you in the heavens—things that cannot be taken away, riches that cannot be plundered.

C   But is your body poorly suited for enduring such pains and miseries? And have the plots of your enemies severely weakened you? You are again providing me with reasons to assure you of another great and ineffable gain. For you know, you know clearly, how important it is to bear bodily infirmity nobly, with thanksgiving. This, as I have told you often, is what crowned Lazarus; and this is what confounded the devil in his combats with Job, rendering that one the most brilliant athlete of patient endurance. This it was, more than his love of poverty, or the ravaging of his possessions, or the sudden loss of his children, or the myriad of plots against him, that proclaimed him victor, and put to shame the evil demon, closing his mouth with great success.

D   Therefore, contemplate these things continually, and rejoice, and be glad that you have brought to a finish such a great contest, that you have borne meekly the greatest of trials, giving glory to God who loves mankind, who is able to make everything suddenly disappear, but who allows such things to happen so that this good enterprise might become more brilliant for you. On account of this we do not cease declaring you to be blessed.

E   We rejoice that having been delivered from the juridical pros-
ecutions, as was fitting for you, you have put an end to the charges
brought against you.[1] You did not give up in a cowardly way, neither
did you obstinately insist on things; and neither did you expose
yourself to the tribunals and the evil things ensuing from them.
Rather, taking a middle course, you are reaping the fruit of your
freedom appropriately; and you are showing forth great intelligence,
long-suffering, endurance, and patience, while demonstrating the
complete accuracy of your understanding.

[1]St John is referring to the two times St Olympia was brought before the fiercely
anti-Christian prefect Optatus, on charges of having started the fire that destroyed the
cathedral in Constantinople on the fateful night when John was taken into exile.

From Arabissos,[1] after about eighteen months in exile

Winter, 405–406

1.A You who have shown forth from your youth such wisdom [*phi-* [619]
losophia], and have trampled upon human vanity—how have you
expected to live a life without troubles and without warfare? How is
this possible? For if men who fight against men receive a myriad of
wounds in the contests and the battles, while you have fought against
principalities and powers, against the rulers of this age of darkness,
against the spirits of wickedness,[2] and you have done this nobly, and
have erected great trophies, and in these ways you have put to grief
that savage and accursed demon—how then have you hoped to live
a tranquil life without any cares?

B No, you do not need to be troubled by how many disturbances
there are everywhere, and how many tumults. On the contrary, if
there were none of these things happening, that would indeed be a
cause for wonder. For virtue always has its lot with pain and danger.

---

[1]This was a frontier fortress town about fifty miles northeast of Cucusus, where
St John was taken when fierce Isaurian raiders attacked Cucusus. John described the
perilous situation at Cucusus in a letter to someone else: "Here there is nothing except
butchery, wild confusion, bloodshed, and blazing buildings, with the Isaurians ravaging whatever they come across with sword and fire" (Letter 61; PG 52, 642; quoted in
Kelly, *Golden Mouth*, 259–60). At Aribissos, secure in the fortress above the city, John
"was able one night to sleep undisturbed while three hundred Isaurians temporarily
wreaked havoc in the lower town" (ibid., cf. Letter 135).
[2]Cf. Eph 6.12.

151

You know this from our previous letters, and you have no need to learn it through any others.

And we are not writing these things in order to instruct someone ignorant. For we know that it is not exile, or enduring the loss of one's goods (which for many is unbearable), or insolent treatment, or any other such tribulation that is able to shake you. And if those who have a part in such sufferings become zealous, how much more do those who live in the midst of them! [c] This is why Paul publicly praised, for two reasons, those Hebrews who had believed, saying, "Remember the former days, in which, after you were enlightened, you endured a great combat in the midst of sufferings, both by being yourselves made a spectacle through opprobrium and tribulations, and by taking part in the sufferings endured by others."[3]

Therefore, we are not making this letter long. For no one who encounters someone who has conquered, and has lifted up brilliant trophies, offers that person assistance, but only accolades. For we know how much wisdom [*philosophia*] you demonstrated in the face [620] of what has occurred. We bless you, and we marvel at the patience you have shown all this time, and at the rewards that are laid up for you henceforth.

D   Since we know well that you wish to learn about what concerns us (and I know I have kept silence for a long time), we have been delivered from a grievous malady, though I am still bearing some ill effects from the disease. And while we enjoyed having excellent doctors, the lack of daily necessities lessened the benefit of their treatment. For there was not only the scarcity of medicine, and of other things that could have corrected my stricken body, but I also had to deal with famine and pestilence. And along with all these things, there are the continual attacks by brigands, who spread out along the furthest routes, and who establish their own fortified places, thus bringing great danger for travelers.

[3]Heb 10.32–33.

Andronicus,[4] as it is reported, fell into their hands; yet after having been stripped of everything, he did manage to escape. Therefore, I beseech Your Graciousness [*sou tēn emmeleian*],[5] do not send anyone else to us now. For it is to be feared that if someone comes to us in our exile, that might become the reason and excuse to have him murdered; and you know how much grief that would cause us.

If you can find someone trustworthy who might be sent here for another reason, give us news of your health through him. But let no one be sent solely to give us a message, or to minister to our needs, on account of the fear that I've just mentioned.

[4] One of St Olympia's couriers.
[5] Literally, "gracefulness."

From Cucusus, after about thirty months in exile

End of 406

1.A Nothing strange or unnatural has happened to Your Piety. [621] Rather, it is most natural and reasonable that the succession of trials, one after another, has well-toned the sinews of your soul even more; and the contests have increased your zeal and strength, producing in you much delight. For such is the nature of tribulation: when it befalls a noble and vibrant soul, it bears these results. And just as fire renders gold more pure when brought into contact with it, so when tribulation comes upon golden souls, it renders them more pure, and more proven. Therefore Paul said, "Tribulation works patience, and patience character."[1]

On account of these things we leap for joy, and rejoice; and in this isolation of ours we are reaping the greatest consolation from this courage of yours. And on account of these things we fear nothing, even if you are encompassed with myriads of wolves and great crowds of evildoers. Still, we do pray that the current trials will [622] subside and that other ones will not be added—thus fulfilling the law of our master who commands us to pray that we be not led into temptation.[2]

B But if further trials are permitted to come upon you, we have confidence in your golden soul, which would gather the greatest

[1]Rom 5.3–4.
[2]Cf. Mt 6.13.

wealth thereby. What is the greatest thing that they, who dare every-thing against themselves, can threaten you with? The loss of your possessions? But I know that you consider all these things to be but dust, and more paltry than mud. What about being exiled from one's country and home? But you know how to dwell in great, very populous cities just as if they were a wilderness—abiding in quietude [*hēsychia*], free from cares the whole time, and trampling upon the fantasies of this earthly life. But what if they threaten you with death? But you have anticipated this, you have meditated upon this cease-lessly; so that if they drag you to be sacrificed, it will be as if they are dragging a corpse.

c   What more is necessary to be said? No one is able to devise anything against you without finding the great abundance of your patience that has been established in you for a long time. For you have always trod the narrow and straitened path, training yourself in all these things. Therefore, having practiced [*askēsasa*][3] this most excellent art in the "gymnasia,"[4] you are now manifesting yourself to be more brilliant, not only by being not at all troubled by what's happening, but by spreading your wings, leaping for joy and danc-ing. For having been trained in the "gymnasia" [through enduring previous trials], you are handling these present contests with great ease. And with a woman's body, weaker than a spider's web, you have trampled with derisive scorn on the madness of men grinding their teeth in fury, and you are ready to suffer even more things than what they are preparing for you.

d   Blessed, and thrice-blessed, are you, due to the crowns that await you—or rather, due to the battles themselves. For such is the

[3]The English word *ascesis* comes from this Greek word.

[4]Classical *gymnasia* were training centers where young male athletes would gather to train for public competitions. The name comes from the Greek word *gymnos* ("naked"), because athletes trained and competed naked. Chrysostom uses the image of "stripping" for the contest several times in these letters (Letter 8.6.d; 8.7.c; 8.9.b; 12.1.b [cf. 8.11.d]).

nature of these contests, that even before the prizes are won, in the midst of the arena, they have their recompense and reward. The delight which you are enjoying now, and the happiness, the courage, the endurance, the patience, the impregnability, the invincibility, and being higher than all [earthly] things, and that you have trained [*askēsai*] yourself in such a way that you cannot be made to suffer from any frightful thing brought on by anyone, and that you stand on a rock in the midst of the billowing waves of a raging sea, sailing with fair breezes with perfect serenity—such are the rewards of tribulations here and now, even before the kingdom of heaven.

E   For I know, I know that being elated with delight, you already consider yourself to be no longer clothed with a body. And when the right time comes, you will shed your body more easily than others take off the garments that clothe them.

Rejoice, therefore, and be glad—for your own sake, and for the sake of those who are blessed to complete their end not in their own beds, neither in their own homes, but in prisons, in chains, in tortures. Grieve only for those who are doing these things [to the innocent], and weep. For this is worthy of your wisdom [*philosophia*].

Since you desire to learn about my bodily health, we have been delivered from the malady that afflicted us recently, and we are getting on better now—unless the approaching winter again aggravates [623] the weakness of our stomach. And as for the Isaurians, we have been settled here in great security.

From Cucusus, after about thirty-two months in exile

Near the beginning of 407

1.A Even with the exceeding severity of the winter, and our stom- [590] ach's infirmity, and the raiding of the Isaurians, do not let your cares for us make you overly anxious. For the winter has been simply what it naturally is in Armenia, so it's not necessary to say anything more about it; and it's not harming us very much.

Foreseeing these things, we have devised many ways to fend off being harmed—having a fire burning continually, having the little room where we're staying screened off all the way around, being wrapped in many blankets, and staying inside all the time. All of this causes us to suffer, but it's bearable because of the beneficial results. For as long as we stay indoors, we are not overly tormented by the cold; but when we are forced to go outside even for a little while, coming into contact with the air, not a little damage is inflicted upon us.

Therefore I beseech Your Excellency, asking for a great favor— that you take great care to amend the infirmity of *your* body. [B] For despondency can produce physical illness; and when the body is in pain and great weakness, when it is completely neglected, and when it is deprived of doctors, temperate weather, and an abundance of daily necessities, consider how not a little aggravation of distress is caused thereby.

Therefore I beg Your Excellency to have recourse to various experienced doctors and such medicines as can rectify your condition. Several days ago, I was vomiting due to the severe weather, and had to employ another remedy—a medicine which was sent to us by my lady the most decorous Synkletia, which healed the malady within three days. I beseech you, therefore, to make use of this remedy yourself, and arrange to send some more of it to us.

c   For when I again began to sense the upset coming, I used the medicine again and was completely healed. For it calms the internal inflammation, it provokes sweating, it provides a moderate degree [591] of warmth, it induces a more than ordinary vigor, and it stirs one's appetite for food. All these things I experienced in the course of a few days. Therefore, please request my venerable lord the count Theophilus to prepare some more of it and send it to us.

d   So do not grieve over how we're spending the winter here. For we are getting along more easily, with better health, than we were a year ago. And you yourself—if you would take care of yourself as you ought to, you would get along much better. But if you say that your maladies are the result of your despondency, why do you still seek letters from us, if they have not contributed to your happiness—and if indeed you have been plunged under the tyranny of despair to such an extent that you now wish to depart from this life?

e   Do you not know how much reward infirmity can bring to a thankful soul? Have I not spoken often on this subject, both in person and in my letters? But if the crowd of cares, or the nature of this infirmity of yours, or everything else coming upon you one after another, do not allow you to hold continuously in your mind the things we have said to you, listen again to us singing this refrain for the healing of the wounds of your despair; as he [St Paul] says, "For to me to write the same things is not troublesome, and for you it provides safety."[1]

    [1]Phil 3.1.

2.A What, therefore, do I say and write? That nothing, Olympia, is so worthy of consideration as *patience* in the midst of pain and grief. For this is the queen of good things, the perfection of crowns, and just as it surpasses other virtues, so this particular form of virtue especially surpasses the others in brilliance.

Perhaps what we've said is not clear—so I will make it clearer. What, therefore, is it that I'm saying? That neither being stripped of one's goods, nor the despoiling of everything that one has, nor falling from a place of honor, nor being driven from one's homeland and carried off to a foreign land, nor being exhausted by pain and sweaty toil, nor dwelling in a prison and being bound by chains, nor reproaches, nor abuses, nor mockeries, nor the loss of one's children—even if all of them are snatched from us suddenly—nor continually menacing enemies, nor anything else like such things; and not even the chief of everything that appears grievous—death itself, so fearsome and terrifying—is as oppressive as bodily illness (even such a great man as Jeremiah was not shaken as much by such things as by bodily affliction)[2]—and yet we still must consider it not a small thing to bear such things nobly, to be an image of endurance.

B   For Job, that great athlete of patience, demonstrates these things, in that when he was afflicted with a bodily disease, he considered death to be a deliverance from the evils that were befalling him. And when he suffered all the other things, he was not as weakened as when he received the bodily blows, one after another, which he considered to be his end. And this was not something small; rather, it was the most grievous of all the wickedness making war against him—being too weak to endure the struggles as he had done at first. For having already fought against the onslaught of arrows being shot at him, then he was given [what seemed to be] a mortal blow—that blow that struck his children, who were taken in such a grievous manner, with both his sons and daughters destroyed all of a sudden,

[2]Cf. Jer 15.18.

[592]   while in the bloom of their youth, and meeting such a violent death that included their burial.[3]

For he neither saw them laid upon a bed, nor did he kiss their hands, nor hear their last words, nor touch their feet and their knees, nor shut their mouths, nor close their eyes when they were about to die—all the things that are not a little comforting to parents who are being separated from their children. Neither did he accompany some of his children to their grave, nor did he find any children remaining to console him for those who had been taken away. For he heard that while they were reclining on couches at a banquet—not a banquet of drunkenness, but of overflowing brotherly love—everything was destroyed and mingled together: the blood, the wine, the cups, the ceiling, the table, the dust, the limbs of his children.

Nevertheless, when he heard about these things, and about the other calamitous things before these, announced by the messenger of evil as in a tragedy—the grievous destruction of the little flocks of sheep and the whole herds of oxen, with the former being destroyed by fire from above, and the latter being seized by plundering enemies and cut in pieces, along with the servants,[4] [c] and seeing such a storm in a brief moment suddenly befalling his fields, his houses, his flocks, his children—with these waves coming one after the other continually—and the crags, and the profound darkness, and the unbearable surging sea—still he was not overcome with despair. Neither did he even deeply feel all that was happening—and that, only in the measure to which he was a man and a father. But when he was handed over to a disease with its sores, then he sought death, then he groaned, then he lamented—so that you might learn that this is more grievous than everything else, and that it gives occasion for the highest form of patience.

And neither is the wicked demon ignorant of this; but having worked all those things upon him, and seeing the athlete remaining

---

[3]They were buried in the rubble when their house collapsed upon them (Job 1.18–19).
   [4]Job 1.13–17.

unmoved and untroubled, he rushed upon him with this supreme test, saying, "For everything is bearable, even the loss of one's children and one's possessions and everything else, except the mortal wound, when one receives pain in his body"—for this is what is meant by "skin for skin."[5] This is why, having been overcome in this contest, the devil did not utter a word, even though previously he had spoken against Job most impudently. And now he did not find any further insolent thing to do; rather, he kept himself far off, and remained hidden.

3.A But do not think of this as an excuse for you also to desire your end, even if that one did desire death, feeling that he could not bear the physical pain. Consider *when* that one desired death, and what the surrounding circumstances were. For he lived before the law was given, before the prophets appeared, before grace had been poured out, and without having partaken of any other kind of philosophy. That we have much greater responsibilities demanded of us than [593] those living back then, and that the arena which is spread out before us is greater, listen to Christ saying, "if your righteousness does not exceed that of the scribes and the Pharisees, you will not enter into the kingdom of heaven."[6]

So, therefore, do not think now that praying for your end is exempt from reproach. Rather, hearken to the voice of Paul saying, "to depart and be with Christ would be far better; but it is more needful for me to remain in the flesh for your sake."[7] For the more the trials increase, the more the crowns abound; and the more the gold is refined by fire, the more it becomes purified; and the longer the merchant sails over the sea, the more merchandise he amasses.

B Do not, therefore, imagine that the struggle now set before you is small; for dealing with bodily illness is more exalted a contest than

[5]Job 2.4.
[6]Mt 5.20.
[7]Phil 1.23–24.

all the things that you have endured, as I have said. For in the case of Lazarus (and while I have said this often to you, nothing prevents me from doing so now), this was enough for his salvation. For simply by bearing—with serenity—poverty, and illness, and the lack of bene- factors, Lazarus departed to the bosom of the one who possessed a house that he shared with all who passed by,[8] who was constantly wandering by the command of God, who sacrificed his own son, the only-begotten one, whom he was given in his extreme old age. It is of such great benefit to those who bear such things nobly that even if one is found who has committed grave sins, this delivers him from the heaviest burden of those sins. And if the person is virtuous and righteous, this adds not a little to his exceedingly great confidence [before the Lord].

c   This is, for the righteous, a brilliant crown, shining more exceedingly than the sun; and for those who have sinned, it is the greatest means of purification. This is why, for the one who had ruined the marriage of his father, who had corrupted his father's marriage-bed, Paul handed him over to the mortification of his flesh, that he might be cleansed in this way. That this was a purification from that disgrace, listen to Paul saying, "that his spirit might be saved in the day of our Lord Jesus Christ."[9] And when in reproaching others for another most fearful sin—that of tasting unworthily of the holy table and those ineffable mysteries (he says that such people are "guilty of the body and blood of the Lord"[10])—behold how he says that they were purified from this grievous impurity: "On account of this many among you are weak and sick."[11] Then, showing that they were no longer bearing the punishment for those things, but were gaining a profit from it, such that they were being delivered from the account due for that sin, he added, "If we judge ourselves, we will not

[8]For "the bosom of Abraham" see Lk 16.22–23; "a house that he shared" refers to the acclaimed hospitality of Abraham (cf. Gen 18.1–15).

[9]1 Cor 5.5.

[10]1 Cor 11.27.

[11]1 Cor 11.30.

be judged; but now if we are judged by the Lord, we are corrected, so that we will not be condemned with the world."[12]

That those who have accomplished great deeds of virtue are making a great gain [from such chastisement], let us learn from Job, who shone forth with great brilliance; and from Timothy, who was so excellent and who fulfilled such a noteworthy ministry, who went with Paul across the whole world—and who, not for just two or [594] three days, or ten or twenty or a hundred, but for many days, lived continually in sickness, with a body greatly weakened. This Paul demonstrates when he says, "Take a little wine for your stomach's sake and your frequent infirmities."[13] This one—who raised people from the dead—did not heal Timothy of his infirmity, but left him in the furnace of illness, so that he might gain thereby a great wealth of confidence.

D   For the one who had enjoyed the company of the master, and had been taught by him, now taught these things to his disciple. If illness did not befall him, trials no less formidable than illness did buffet him, causing him to suffer great pain in his flesh: "For a thorn in the flesh was given to me by a messenger of Satan," he says, "in order to buffet me"[14]—indicating by this the blows, the bonds, the chains, the prisons, being led away, being savagely attacked, being struck often with whips by public torturers. And because he was not bearing [well] the pains in his flesh that these things caused, he said, "I besought the Lord three times ('three times' meaning many times) so that I might be delivered from this thorn."[15] Then, since he did not obtain what he asked for, and since he learned of the advantage thereby, he kept silent, and rejoiced in what had happened.

E   And you, therefore, if you stay in your house, if you are held fast in your bed, do not think that you are living an unproductive life.

[12]1 Cor 11.31–32.
[13]1 Tim 5.23. Chrysostom devotes his first homily "On the Statues" to this verse.
[14]2 Cor 12.7.
[15]2 Cor 12.8.

For you are enduring something *more grievous* than what you have suffered at the hands of public torturers, by whom you have been dragged, savagely attacked, stretched to the utmost—and that is this extreme infirmity of yours, which is like having a public torturer continually residing in your house. But do not therefore either desire your end or neglect your health; for that is not safe. Therefore Paul heartily advises Timothy to take the greatest care of himself. But about your illness—it's enough to say these things.

4.A If it is being separated from us that causes your despondency, expect to be freed from this. And I don't say this now just to comfort you, but because I know that this surely will happen. If it were not meant to be, I think I should long ago have been set free from this life here below, considering the trials which have been inflicted upon me.

Passing over what happened in Constantinople after my departure from there, you understand what I endured on that long and tortuous journey—which in itself was sufficient to bring death—and then after my arrival here, then after my departure from Cucusus, and then after my sojourn in Arabissos.[16]

B   But we have escaped all of that, and now we are in good health and much security—to such an extent that all the Armenians are [595] astonished that in such a weak body, like a spider's web, I am bearing unbearable cold, and that I am even able to breathe, when those who are used to living here are having such a difficult time enduring the severity of the winter.

But we are abiding uninjured up to the present time, having escaped from the hands of brigands who have often come upon us, and surviving a privation of daily necessities, and not being able to take a bath. And while all along during our exile we have lived in this way, feeling a continual need for a bath, now we are so well estab-

---

[16]A fortress town to the northeast where he was kept for a brief time. See footnote 1 on p. 151.

lished that we do not even desire the consolation that would come from that, as we are now abiding in greater health.

And neither the inclemency of the weather, nor the desolation of the region, nor the scarcity of goods, nor the dearth of attendants, nor the unskillfulness of the doctors, nor the absence of baths, nor being confined all day long to one room as in a prison, nor being continually unable to move even when I have need to do so, nor constantly abiding in the smoke and near the fire, nor the fear of robbers nor their ceaseless raids, nor any other similar thing has prevailed over us. Indeed, we are getting along in better health than previously, when we were receiving much care for our health.

In considering all of this, drive away the despondency that now envelopes you, and do not inflict exaggerated and grievous punishments on yourself. [c] I have sent you what I wrote recently on the topic that "no one can harm the one who does not injure himself."[17] The discourse that I am now sending Your Excellency fights the same battle. Therefore, it is needful for you to read through it constantly. And if you are healthy enough, read it aloud. For it will be a medicine sufficient for you, if you wish it to be.[18]

But if you strive against us, neither healing yourself nor wishing to bring yourself out of the stagnant waters of despair, even though you are enjoying an abundance of advice and exhortation from us, then it will not be easy for us to consent to send you numerous, long letters, as long as you are not about to gain anything from them for your happiness.

D   How then will we know this? Not by what you say, but by what you show forth with your deeds, since you have said recently that

[17]This is the exact name of the treatise translated in NPNF¹ 9:271–84. It is also published in a French translation, with the original Greek, in SC 103, under the title *Lettre d'Exil.*

[18]This second discourse is most likely the one known as *On the Providence of God*, which appears in Greek and French in SC 79. An English translation of this treatise has recently been published: St. John Chrysostom, *On the Providence of God*, Monk Moses (Worcester), trans. (Platina, CA: St. Herman of Alaska Brotherhood, 2015).

nothing else but your despondency is what has caused this illness. Since, therefore, you have confessed this yourself, if you do not free yourself from this infirmity, we will not believe that you have been delivered from the despondency. For if this [despondency] is indeed the cause of your illness, just as you have written to us, it is very evident that if one is removed the other will be terminated with it; and with the root being pulled up, the branches will be destroyed as well. But as long as flowers remain and flourish, and unwelcome fruit is being borne, we will not believe that you have been freed from the root of your distress. Therefore, do not bring forth more words to me, but show forth actions; and if you get well, you will see once again letters from me discoursing in overflowing measure.

E   Do not consider it only a small consolation that we are alive, that we are in good health, that having been encompassed with so many difficulties, we have been delivered from sickness and infirmity—on account of which our enemies, who know this, are in exceeding grief and pain. It follows, therefore, that this should be your greatest [596] encouragement, and your chief consolation. And do not call your life-journey a desolation, for it is already inscribed in the heavens through the sufferings that you are enduring.

F   I have suffered much pain on account of the monk Pelagius.[19] Consider therefore what crowns those will be worthy of who stand nobly, while [some] men who live in such asceticism and persever-ance are being dragged down to perdition.

---

[19]This is most likely not the infamous founder of the Pelagian heresy that arose in Rome through the teachings of a British monk named Pelagius, since that Pelagius was still respected in Rome until the year 409.

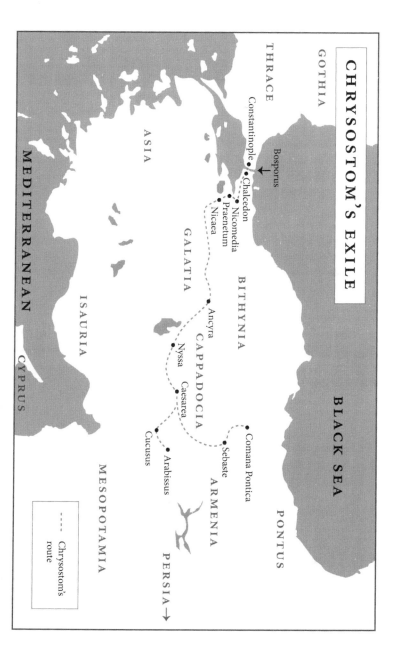

CHRYSOSTOM'S EXILE

GOTHIA

THRACE

Constantinople

Bosporus

ASIA

Chalcedon
Nicomedia
Praenetum
Nicaea

BITHYNIA

GALATIA

Ancyra

CAPPADOCIA

Nyssa

Caesarea

ISAURIA

Comana Pontica

Sebaste

Cucusus

Arabissus

ARMENIA

MEDITERRANEAN

CYPRUS

MESOPOTAMIA

PERSIA →

BLACK SEA

PONTUS

---- Chrysostom's route

POPULAR PATRISTICS SERIES

ST VLADIMIR'S SEMINARY PRESS
1-800-204-2665 • www.svspress.com